OUTSIDE
OF YOUR
HEAD

OUTSIDE OF YOUR HEAD

NIKOLINA KOSANOVIC

NEW DEGREE PRESS
COPYRIGHT © 2020 NIKOLINA KOSANOVIC
All rights reserved.

OUTSIDE OF YOUR HEAD

ISBN   978-1-64137-967-0   *Paperback*
       978-1-64137-796-6   *Kindle Ebook*
       978-1-64137-797-3   *Ebook*

*This book is dedicated to everyone living with
an unwanted friend in their head.*

CONTENTS

	INTRODUCTION	11

	BACKGROUND	**19**
I.	THE BRAIN 101	21
II.	YOU AGAINST THE WORLD	31
III.	STIGMA AND SURVIVAL	41
IV.	SOON YOU'LL GET BETTER: THE TOOLS	49
	A CONNECTION (WITH ME)	59

	ACCEPT	**65**
I.	'ACCEPT' INTRODUCTION	67
II.	THE WORLD DOESN'T REVOLVE AROUND ME	69
III.	YOU'RE NEVER GOING TO BE 'THE BEST': RELATIONSHIPS WITH FAILURE	77
IV.	SOMETIMES, YOU HAVE BAD TIMING	85
V.	PEOPLE HAVE RIGHTS, AND YES, IT'S INCONVENIENT	91
VI.	YOU CAN'T CONTROL EVERYTHING	99
VII.	SELF-CARE REQUIRES SACRIFICE	105
VIII.	KINDNESS IS THE ANSWER, BUT THAT DOESN'T ALWAYS MEAN BEING NICE	111
IX.	THIS TOO SHALL PASS	119
X.	FRIENDS MAY SAY THEY WANT THE WORLD FOR YOU, BUT ONLY IF IT'S ONE THEY CAN ENVISION	125
XI.	PEOPLE WILL LEAVE YOUR LIFE, AND FIGHTING IT WILL DO MORE HARM THAN GOOD	131
	A CONNECTION (ACCEPT TO REFLECT)	137

	REFLECT	**143**
I.	'REFLECT' INTRODUCTION	145
II.	'A BIG FAT PHONY'	147
III.	THE IMPORTANCE OF CONTEXT	159
IV.	SEARCHING FOR HAPPINESS	169
V.	A BROKEN BONE AND THE ART OF HEALING	177
VI.	A NOTE ABOUT ACCOUNTABILITY	185
VII.	REFLECTIONS ON ANGER	193
VIII.	FORGIVENESS: THE DOOR THAT OPENS	201
IX.	REFLECTIONS ON YOURSELF: THE OTHER HALF OF FORGIVENESS	209
	A CONNECTION (REFLECT TO EMBRACE)	221

	EMBRACE	**229**
I.	'EMBRACE' INTRODUCTION	231
II.	EMBRACING THE DARK SIDE: THE BENEFIT OF COMEDY	233
III.	DEPRESSION AND EMPATHY	237
IV.	THE ANXIOUS CREATIVE	241
V.	OCD AND GREAT WORK	245
VI.	SHUTTING DOWN AND PATIENCE	251
VII.	(FAUX BUT) FEARLESS	257
VIII.	BEING YOUR OWN BEST FRIEND	263
	A CONNECTION (WITH YOU)	267
	ACKNOWLEDGMENTS	269
	APPENDIX	275

"Remember in the depth and even the agony of despondency, that very shortly you are to feel well again."

ABRAHAM LINCOLN, 1842

INTRODUCTION

Everyone has a "first," that "first" being an experience that exposes you to some type of pain or struggle that a segment of the population is subjected to suffer through. It's something that bursts the bubble of the world you've imagined and shatters the illusion and prejudice you held before. You may have your perspective opened and changed many times throughout your life, but it's the first one that cuts you the deepest, and often comes when you least expect it.

Waves were crashing into the sand and accompanying the sound of seagulls singing, my family laughing, and the pop of the Brisk can I had just opened when my "first" happened to me. It happened to me on, what was supposed to be, yet another family beach day.

Growing up on the Gulf Coast of Florida, these family trips to the beach were a staple of my childhood. For a working-class family, it was affordable and it allowed the entire family to get together. In fact, the one and only vacation I remember us taking as a family when I was young included driving to the other the side of the state to enjoy the Atlantic's version of our ever-familiar beach day.

"What a nice change in scenery," I remember my brother jokingly responding when my parents told us to pack for the trip. My parents got him back for his sarcasm when we got there by planting seaweed on his back when he wasn't looking and watching him leap out of the water in Olympic-qualifiable time.

Despite all the positive memories I made at the beach over the years, it, like everything else, provided unpleasant ones as well. Between almost losing a finger while being attacked by a flock of seagulls over a ham sandwich, all the stingrays and jellyfish that attempted to poison me on numerous occasions, and all the no-contact bumper cars we were forced to play in parking lots with the hundreds of angry tourists, it sometimes felt like I was a contestant on *Survivor*. But my "first" didn't involve any of those scenarios.

I was little, around five years old, lying on a blue floating bed in the water next to a few of my standing adult family members. The sunlight was mercilessly beating on me, and my skin and floaties were rendered uncomfortably dry. I decided to start taking off my floaties before their dry plastic ends could scratch my skin, and I successfully got the first one off. While working on the second one, however, I lost my balance on the floating bed and I fell into the ocean.

I started violently kicking, but I was barely able to pop my head up for air. Being disproportionately more buoyant on the side with the remaining floatie, my efforts were proving futile, and I was quickly losing oxygen. Finally, I stopped kicking, and I remember looking up through the salty water and seeing the blurry bright sky. In that moment, I thought of nothing.

I remember the feeling of being so small. The water was shallow enough that my parents could easily stand in it, and yet here I was next to them drowning. How could I be so close yet so disconnected? How could one floatie not be enough to at least help me get my head above the water?

It wasn't more than a few seconds later that I felt the sweet relief of a hand grab me and throw me back onto the safety of the blue floating bed. Someone realized that what seemed like a little kid playing in the water was actually me fighting for my life.

Grateful, I took in a few deep breaths and stared again at the clear bright sky. With lungs that were coughing out the water that nearly suffocated them just a few seconds earlier, and a body that was aching from the fight, my mind was reeling to process it all.

"Are you okay?" my mom asked as she used her thumb to brush wet hair out of my face.

"Yeah," I managed to muster out, and that was the last thing I said for a good while. I spent the next twenty minutes laying on the bed, shriveling up, and processing the extremely unexpected turn of events. All the while, I clutched to the dear sense of safety that refusing to remove the increasingly uncomfortable floaties provided me.

The memory of that day depicts what it's like to live a life plagued by depression.

It starts like any other day. Imagine enjoying your favorite latte, a healthy breakfast, or even good news when, suddenly, you're knocked over into an overwhelming sea of feelings. You're immediately suffocating, and after a few kicks, you sink into obedience as memories, insults, and fear are flashed for your viewing displeasure.

You become so small that what seemed like a shallow body of water, feels miles away from any family, friends, or help available to you, even if they're only physically a few feet away. The world becomes blurry, meaningless, and numbing until a hand grabs you and pulls you out of the sea.

When you're on the other side of its debilitating grasp, you begin your recovery as you clutch onto whatever pretense of safety you have in that moment. Healing is a slow journey. That day on the beach may have been my "first," but it was only the beginning of a lifetime of drowning in the sea of depression.

After a lifetime of fighting, I started to wonder if there was a better way to face the issue.

Mental illness is everywhere, and to the untrained eye, it can go unnoticed. We live in an increasingly individualistic society that continuously places binary labels on complex topics. We simplify many things into these categories of being "good" or "bad," "happy" or "sad," "grateful" or "ungrateful." We even go a step further and begin to link the categories (often inappropriately) to one another. For example, we can link being "sad," with being "bad," often adding stigma and shame to the feeling.

As this phenomenon becomes more commonplace, it slowly shifts our perception to begin viewing the world at a surface level. This mindset affects how we interact. We stop asking questions when we categorize our lives into these simple buckets, and in turn, we miss opportunities to better understand and support each other in the process. This labeling is particularly harmful when we start to put people into these binary categories.

Think of the "eccentric" friend we know who posts on their social media page hourly. We assume they're happy, but neglect to ask why they're posting so much. If we did, we'd find out because they're trying to hide some of the personal tragedies they're going through by showing a different face to their social media friends.

Then there's the "successful" employee who you think of as an overachiever. They're constantly working and they seem to love their job, but the "why" behind their workaholism is actually them trying to fill the void left by the loss of their pregnancy to a miscarriage.

Then there's the "skinny" family member who we envy after they've lost "all that weight." But what we neglected to ask was "how." When we do, we find they suffered from a terrible eating disorder after their long-term relationship ended that caused them to puke it all off.

The hardest part of this is that these people don't even ask themselves "why." They simply survive. But without the reflection and support that would come from others trying to understand the complexity behind their actions, they repress and move on…often causing their issues to become recurring.

Globally, the World Health Organization (WHO) states that more than 264 million people suffer from depression.[1] However, depression is only one ailment on a long list of diagnosable mental illnesses, and a diagnosis is not a prerequisite for the suffering they cause.

We're all suffering in our own ways. But, more often than not, we're doing it alone, even though we shouldn't have to.

I've spent my life struggling with mental illness, and I've tried a lot of traditional methods of treatment to try to "cure" myself, but nothing has ever fully worked. What I've learned from these experiences is that my depression (the most potent

---

[1] "Depression." World Health Organization, World Health Organization, accessed on April 30, 2020.

part of my mental illness) is a part of me, and the goal is to learn to successfully manage it while gaining tools and lessons from every single episode. No "cure" has been found, and searching for one has made me feel defeated and like a failure when I was already at my lowest.

Mental illness subjects a person's brain to adopting a different way of functioning. Even if you "cure" one symptom of the illness, you'll find that it often manifests itself into another form. In my life, I've seen this manifestation transition among symptoms, behaviors, and lifestyle choices. One such example is how I used to get terrible headaches from anger in response to high-emotional events. Nowadays, the same events prompt anxiety-fueled stomach pains.

The question should not be how to "cure" mental illness, but rather how to best "manage" the symptoms. Because once we learn how to properly manage it, we can lower the chances of it negatively impacting our lives and even learn to embrace and value certain skills that come out of dealing with the darkness.

Though the symptoms themselves aren't always a good thing, the skills we learn from them absolutely can be. In my life, I've seen some of the skills I've honed to manage my depressive and hypomanic episodes be the biggest contributors to my successes. It can be hard to look at it in this positive perspective, especially when dealing with your mental illness is a personal and daily struggle. It's even harder to do so when the world keeps telling you there's something wrong with you, and it's your fault for not curing it yet.

This book is the culmination of the experiences and lessons I've learned, focusing on the specific ailments of bipolar disorder, depression, and anxiety, which are my own personal afflictions. More specifically, it is an empirical piece on what mental illness means in our society and changing the mindset with which we view it and how we approach living with it in ourselves.

We break down this approach into four main sections:

1. **Background** discusses the technical pieces of mental illness and our society.
2. **Accept** talks about lessons I've learned and accepted that have helped me manage my inner self-talk during symptomatic episodes.
3. **Reflect** dives into different themes and emotions affected by mental illness. This section aims to answer some of the "why" behind the feelings in the journey of healing.
4. **Embrace** looks at some of the valuable skills that can be learned in the journey of dealing with mental illness and ends our literary adventure with positive perspectives that can serve as takeaways in changing the mindset with which the world views mental illness.

Mental illness is often misunderstood as a "phase" or something that's "all in your head." But for many who live their lives with it, it's a lot like the unexpected drowning memory I'll always have with me. You can't control it, but you can learn from it. And like the memory, it'll always be with you.

These pages are my journey of accepting, reflecting on, and embracing this statement. Through them, I hope you can learn to better live with the misunderstood friend in your head.

BACKGROUND

I.

THE BRAIN 101

No organ in our body is more misunderstood than the brain. So, it comes as no surprise that something so misunderstood is behind the ominous feelings and mental illnesses on which we as a society are deeply uneducated. Before we can dive into better understanding mental illness, we need to understand the basics of the science behind the brain. While you may not walk out of this chapter a neuroscientist, you will at the very least gain some newfound knowledge behind the organ that stores it all.

DIFFERENT TYPES OF STUDIES ON THE BRAIN
The connection between the body and the mind is an important, yet universally misunderstood, concept. At their core, all of our emotions have a physical link in our body to which they can be traced. Yet, pairing something as abstract as emotions with something as scientific as our biological composition has proven quite difficult. Even with the knowledge that this connection exists, science has yet to paint a clear picture of the inner workings of the brain.

At their core, there are two divisions of all the specialized brain sciences: neurology and psychology. Their differences are based on what they study. Neurology focuses on studying the structure of the nervous system, while psychology focuses on studying our human mind and behavior.[2] [3]

Though they have different focuses and methods to their research, their studies overlap. Most importantly, their goal to help people afflicted by symptoms they can't understand are, at their core, the same. Thus, the fields benefit greatly from collaboration, and this collaboration is pivotal to helping all of us individually manage our symptoms.

THE AREAS OF THE BRAIN

The brain in its totality is composed of billions of nerves with trillions of connections, known as synapses.[4] To make its composition a tad more palatable, we can break it down into four main sections, as illustrated below.

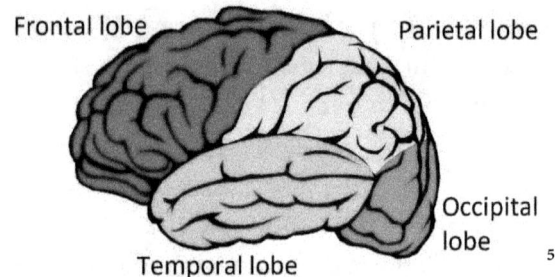
[5]

---

2   *Merriam-Webster*, s.v. "neurology (_n._)," accessed April 30, 2020.
3   *Merriam-Webster*, s.v. "psychology (_n._)," accessed April 30, 2020.
4   Matthew Hoffman, MD, "Picture of the Brain: Human Anatomy," WebMD, accessed on May 18, 2020.
5   Nisheeth Shah. *Left and Right Neural Networks—Inspired by Our Bicameral Brains*. ResearchGate, 2019 fig. 2. (2019).

These lobes interact with each other to execute our daily functions. However, they are also specialized to focus on their own roles in our functioning.

- The *frontal lobe* is associated with the problem solving, judgment, and motor function of an individual.[6]
- The *parietal lobe* is associated with the managing of our senses, including awareness, depth perception, handwriting, and the ability to differentiate between our left and our right.[7]
- The *temporal lobe* controls our aural perception, languages, and most aspects of memory.[8]
- The *occipital lobe* is responsible for visual processing.[9]

Another two relevant parts of the brain are the following:

- The *insula* is a part of our brain that integrates aspects of languages, pain, temperature processing, and, as some also speculate, taste.[10]
- The *limbic system* is primarily responsible for the processing of our six primary emotions, feelings of pleasure, and many aspects of social behavior.[11]

---

6 Juebin Huang, MD, PhD, "Overview of Cerebral Function—Neurologic Disorders," Merck Manuals Professional Edition. Merck Manuals, accessed on May 1, 2020.
7 Ibid.
8 Ibid.
9 Ibid.
10 Ibid.
11 Ibid.

Though this book won't go into much of the scientific knowledge and research of these areas of the brain, a basic understanding is important for those who are trying to relate their emotions and mental patterns to tangible physical areas within the body. Any chemical changes in these areas of the brain can quickly alter the functions they control. Thus, if there's any type of imbalance in the brain, the entire body and its daily functions will be affected.

THE SIX BASIC EMOTIONS
Scientists believe there are six basic emotions, from which all our more complex emotions stem. These emotions are linked to physical areas in the brain, specifically the limbic system, which is defined above.[12] The six basic emotions are happiness, fear, sadness, disgust, anger, and surprise.[13] All of our other emotions are believed to be a combination of any of these six basic emotions, similar to how the three primary colors combine to create every other color known to the visible eye.

Though there is a tangible place that acts as the source of our emotions, they are subjective in how they feel for everyone, and they can even change as certain events and traumas change the brain.

HOW TRAUMA CHANGES THE BRAIN
Trauma activates the part of our brain that focuses on survival. During this activation, our body undergoes the stress

---

12 R.L. Isaacson, "Limbic System," ScienceDirect Topics, International Encyclopedia of the Social & Behavioral Sciences, accessed on May 1, 2020.

13 Heidi Moawad, MD, "How the Brain Processes Emotions," Neurology Times, MJH Life Sciences, June 5, 2017.

response needed to prep us for our "fight or flight" decision. After this decision is made, the stress dissipates, and normal functioning levels return. But for some, the normal functioning never truly returns, and they are left in a perpetual state of stress. This perpetual stress on the brain can change which emotions are triggered in response to an event. As a result, someone who may have reacted one way to a situation may react in a completely different way once they've experienced a trauma that never allowed their system to return to pre-trauma levels.[14]

For example, someone who was bullied as a child may have a very hard time processing jokes at their expense in a group setting. Because these jokes trigger the traumatic feelings the bullies instilled in them, they may quickly get angry in response to the joke and be unable to talk themselves out of their anger. This reaction happens because the joke triggers the trauma, and the person's focus for survival makes them lash out.

Another example could be someone who survived a war in which they were around many bomb explosions. This person may have a hard time processing loud noises. They may shut down, they may have a panic attack, or they may feel a need to run into a quiet space. That's because their brain is wired from the trauma of the bombs to associate these loud noises with impending destruction and death, even if it's just a DJ at a nightclub.

Trauma is different for everyone, even two people who experience the same event. The types of trauma that can have these altering effects have traditionally been defined

---

14   Michele Rosenthal, "The Science Behind PTSD Symptoms: How Trauma Changes the Brain," PsychCentral, Psych Central, June 27, 2019.

as life-altering events, such as being the victim of rape, surviving a natural disaster, or the sudden death of a loved one. But anything that is unexpected, shocking, or life-altering provides an opportunity for a heightened level of stress that never properly resolves itself. Depending on the values and worldview of the person in question, something as common as a romantic breakup, loss of a job, or dissolution of a friendship can be enough to trigger it.

Understanding that trauma can change the way our brain sends signals can help us understand why we act differently once life changes take place. More importantly, it provides a biological reason that proves our feelings are very valid.

NEUROPLASTICITY

Just like the brain can change with trauma and cause symptoms that negatively impact our ability to perform daily functions, the brain can also change in a positive way. Neuroplasticity is a concept which the Oxford dictionary defines as "the ability of the brain to form and reorganize synaptic connections, especially in response to learning or experience following injury."[15] So, simply put, something like trauma has the ability to change the way our brain functions, but so do many other things. If we're able to control the majority of what we subject our brain to, we can actively subject it to behaviors that reorganize its functions to better fit our goals.

Growing up, I heard a lot of myths about how we begin with a finite number of brain cells and that, every time we hit our head, we lose "x" amount of those brain cells, and that they never grow back. Well, in its earlier days, scientists studying neuroplasticity discovered the ability of stress to

---

15   *Oxford Reference*, s.v. "neuroplasticity (_n._)," accessed on April 20, 2020.

change the brain and kill brain cells. It was assumed that brain cells, once disposed of, could never be regenerated. However, it has been found that there can be opportunities to relearn and reestablish some of those diminished parts of the brain, which can give many of us a brighter outlook when trying to overcome trauma or mental disorders.[16]

When you think about it in the simplest terms, in nature, our goal is to survive. To do this, every part of our body must adapt to our environment, and our brain is no exception. One really good example of neuroplasticity, and its physical connection, is studied in the Moken people. They are a group of "sea gypsies" who live in Asia and have enhanced underwater vision and diving abilities.[17] Many attribute these enhanced abilities to the signals that their brains send to their eyes to constrict their pupils by 22 percent, allowing them to dive at greater lengths.[18]

On a less survival-driven level, something as simple as learning a new dance step involves creating a new neuropathway, which is an example of your brain experiencing neuroplasticity. This example, quite literally, proves that the process of rewiring your brain on a journey of healing must be taken "one step at a time." But the results of connecting

---

16 Courtney E. Ackerman, MSc, "What Is Neuroplasticity? A Psychologist Explains [+14 Exercises]," Body & Brain, PositivePsychology.com, April 28, 2020.

17 Angeline S Lillard and Alev Erisir, "Old Dogs Learning New Tricks: Neuroplasticity Beyond the Juvenile Period," Developmental Review (Volume 31, Issue 4, December 1, 2011), 207–239.

18 Daniel Honan, "Neuroplasticity: You Can Teach an Old Brain New Tricks," Big Think, The Big Think, Inc, October 11, 2012.

those steps can be absolutely profound, just like a well-executed choreography.

BEYOND THE BRAIN

The biological connection to our feelings is not solely limited to the brain. One other strong connection is to the thing we sometimes wish we would listen more to…our gut.

The gut-brain connection isn't a new concept. For myself, and many people in my life, the lack of an appetite or the presence of an upset stomach can be the by-product of depression or anxiety. For a while, I rendered it a mere coincidence, but there is scientific merit to it. Like we mentioned above, the brain is responsible for controlling signals to your body. As such, it will initiate the release of signals to the gut, like preparing you to eat. However, the brain can also send inappropriate signals for the situation, like mentioned above in the note on trauma changing the brain.[19] So if you experience issues with your gut whenever your symptoms take over, you may have inappropriate signals to blame for it.

Another component of the gut's interplay with our emotions has to do with an estimated 90 percent of our body's serotonin being produced in the gut.[20] Serotonin is a neurotransmitter that is linked to both physiological and psychological conditions, including clinical depression, among other things. Many Selective Serotonin Reuptake Inhibitor (SSRI) antidepressants, and even more "natural" solutions like 5-HTP (a precursor to serotonin) supplements, have

---

19 Harvard Health Publishing, "The Gut-Brain Connection," Healthbeat, Harvard University, accessed on May 1, 2020.

20 Jessica Stoller-Conrad, "Microbes Help Produce Serotonin in Gut," Caltech, California Institute of Technology, April 9, 2015.

helped many people manage their mood disorders.[21] However, as we'll come to find through these pages, one tool often needs to be paired with other tools for effective management, because there's more to a mood disorder than the chemical imbalance.

A HOLISTIC VIEW

To understand ourselves, we must understand the mind-body connection. Though this book doesn't aim to do more than touch upon the neuroscience component of what we define as mental illness, it's still important to dedicate some time in our discussion to the brain.

Understanding ourselves starts with our surroundings, which is most easily expressed in what we can touch and feel. Our emotions are more abstract than that, so understanding the physiological parts of our body that fuel our emotions helps us have a more holistic view of our actions and a greater willingness to validate the feelings we experience.

---

21 Colette Bouchez, "Serotonin and Depression: 9 Questions and Answers," WebMD, WebMD LLC, October 12, 2011.

II.

YOU AGAINST THE WORLD

―

Many days, when I wake up, I feel overwhelmed by the challenges thrown at me. They come in the form of deadlines at work, unexpected accidents, and ominous interactions with loved ones. Some days, the challenges feel like more than one person can handle. But despite everything, I find ways to push through, alone, because I feel like that's what's expected of me.

"You're an adult," they say. "Take care of it yourself."

All throughout my life, the world has never ceased to remind me that I'm responsible for my own problems, and, if I want to be successful, I can't expect it to be handed to me. On the contrary, there will always be people trying to ruin it for one reason or another. I've always felt like I've been up against the world, and that no one else could understand what it was like. Little did I know that these feelings of loneliness were a by-product of the culture that surrounded me, and many of the people who seemed "against" me were feeling the same feelings, too.

For those of us living in North America or Western Europe, there's a very good chance we're living in an individualistic culture. Individualistic culture is one defined by independent and autonomous citizens who put more emphasis on their individual needs than on the needs of their community.[22] One of the most individualistic societies is the United States.[23]

The contrary culture to an individualistic society is a collectivist one. A collectivist culture is defined by an emphasis on the needs of a collective group rather than on the needs of an individual within the group. These cultures tend to be found in countries located in Asia, Central America, South America, and Africa.[24]

This book will focus primarily on the individualistic perspective, as I spent the majority of my life in the United States. However, I still hold a collectivistic perspective originating from my background, Eastern European family influence, and early memories. Thus, this chapter will focus on defining the two and exploring some of their influences.

NATURE VERSUS NURTURE

Prior to diving into the specifics of these two cultures, I wanted to revisit a debate that may look very familiar: nature vs. nurture. This debate is something I did numerous projects on at different points throughout grade school. It revolves

---

[22] Kendra Cherry, "Individualistic Cultures and Behavior," Verywell Mind, Dotdash Publishing Family, reviewed on March 24, 2020.

[23] Ava Rosenbaum, "Personal Space and American Individualism," Brown Political Review, Brown University, October 31, 2018.

[24] Kendra Cherry, "Understanding Collectivist Cultures," Verywell Mind, Dotdash Publishing Family, reviewed on March 24, 2020.

around the argument about which factor influences the behavior and outcome of a living being: 1.) nature, aka genetics, or 2.) nurture, aka the environment. The conclusion that my peers and I came to was that both factors play their part in the composition of any living being. But I always believed nurture played a slightly more substantial role in a human's development.

Bringing back the idea of neuroplasticity that we just explored in the previous chapter, we understand that an environment can prompt a person's brain to change the signals it sends to the body. Thus, someone who grows up in an individualistic society can become so used to having to take care of themselves in difficult situations that their brain prompts feelings of discontent anytime they have to share their resources. Alternatively, the pathway in their brain that they would typically use when asking others for help may be blocked. If it's been unsuccessful in the past for their survival, why would the brain focus its signals on it in future events? In these cases, your brain can quite literally make you feel like you're up against the world, prompting loneliness.

On the other hand, the brain of person who grows up supporting the community over their own needs might depend on neuropathways that involve turning to their community in times of personal need. If this avenue fails, they may, subsequently, fail to find another one. In this instance, that person's environment prevented them from becoming resourceful and creative in tackling their issues. This failure can lead one to feel unimportant and unworthy in the eyes of their community, prompting negative feelings that make them feel pessimistic about their place in the world.

Holding the belief that nurture plays a more substantial role in a human's development is important in understanding why our environments are so influential on our mental health. For many of us who suffer from depression and other similar symptoms, feeling lonely and misunderstood can exacerbate the issue and prevent many people from seeking out help. We're only as powerful as what we know, and the world can seem a lot more optimistic when you know why you feel a certain way and what your options are.

INDIVIDUALISTIC CULTURE

One assumption we can make about individualistic cultures is that they tend to be more prominent in what are defined globally as "developed" countries (a definition that typically tends to be based off of productivity and GDP). This trend may be a by-product of the traits that people in individualistic cultures tend to have. Typically, individual rights take center stage, being dependent upon others is shameful, and the desire to be unique in comparison to your peers is omnipresent. Aside from the United States; Germany, South Africa, Ireland, and Australia are also considered to be individualistic societies.[25]

Based on the research, some of my interpretations for why the individualistic cultures tend to be concentrated in wealthier nations are based on the aforementioned traits and behaviors that they promote. For people who are striving to be independent of others, one of the main avenues to achieve this goal is through financial independence. Individual financial independence is more likely to occur in a wealthier nation, especially one where the opportunities for

---

25 Kendra Cherry, "Individualistic Cultures and Behavior," Verywell Mind, Dotdash Publishing Family, reviewed on March 24, 2020.

education and employment can bestow someone with the means to living independently.

In a country like the United States, this outcome is so likely that it becomes expected, and falling short of this expectation can subject one to a high degree of negative social pressure. Just think about how much shame young adults may feel if they're living with their parents after turning eighteen. Though they may be perfectly happy and comfortable doing so, others may make them feel like failures for not paying their own bills.

But this emphasis on independence can be a good thing because, for a culture of people striving to be unique, there is a certain ambition and drive that pushes them to make advances that lead to economic growth and a wealthier nation overall.

When facing hard times, someone in an individualistic society is encouraged to take on their problems by themselves, and may even feel shame turning to their family or friends for assistance.[26] So that pervasive mindset of feeling overwhelmed and lonely throughout life's challenges that I mentioned I feel quite frequently is a by-product of living in this type of environment. This mindset goes even further, as these feelings of loneliness and lack of support can trigger more intense periods of depression and anxiety and prevent someone from getting help because they feel ashamed by the idea of depending on someone else.

---

26 Kendra Cherry, "Individualistic Cultures and Behavior," Verywell Mind, Dotdash Publishing Family, reviewed on March 24, 2020.

COLLECTIVIST CULTURE

Collectivist cultures are ones that may be viewed as more traditional, and in some cases, less socially liberal. Some examples of collectivist countries are Japan, China, Brazil, and India, among many others. A lot of these countries have cultures that encourage citizens to put the needs of their community above their own, praise selflessness, and make families and communities the central part of their citizens' lives.[27]

Though I made the observation that individualistic cultures tend to be synonymous with the wealthiest nations, that is not always the case. For example, Japan is a country that is universally known as being wealthy, with a very high GDP and level of productivity. Japan, however, has a collectivist culture.

For many of these cultures, the importance of the family image to the rest of society is extremely important. The importance of the traditional family unit and structure in their society can be assumed to be part of why these cultures are more traditional. The desire for people to be selfless and see their families and communities as their main motivator is a key component to the survival of their societal structure. As a result, there may not be as much innovation or financial independence on an individual level because of their desire to support their family unit rather than be unique.

However, just like individualistic cultures can feel lonely, someone from a collectivist culture may feel lost if their desires do not fit with their families. Using my own experiences as an example, my family is very loving and

---

27 Kendra Cherry, "Understanding Collectivist Cultures," Verywell Mind, Dotdash Publishing Family, reviewed on March 24, 2020.

supportive, as we come from a very collectivist culture in Serbia. Growing up, my parents would always say that in our home country, a neighbor would never let another neighbor starve, in comparison to living in America. But it can be a double-edged sword, because unconditional support is hard to find, and often, there are strings attached. Sometimes, it's those same neighbors who offer the helping hand that expect something in return for it, and judge the hardest if you fail to meet those expectations.

In a collectivist culture, if you find that you do not fit the mold of what is expected of you from your family or your culture, there is a sense of opposition and ostracizing. The demands of others are felt more than they would be in an individualistic culture, and to cater to them, you may be asked to repress your desires for others' sake. Sometimes, putting others first can be extremely detrimental to the mental health of someone growing up, or at least they were for me. But I also knew that if I ever needed my family, they would rally an army to support me, and that kind of mentality can truly help anyone get back on their feet.

BEHAVIOR

Aside from the assumptions made above, there are some studied observations that show trends of how people behave based on which of these cultures they're from. In a collectivist culture, harmony with the social group and acceptance within a community are the most important things to have. As a result, people in these societies tend to have more social anxiety and less open and communicative relationships out of fear of saying things that will hurt their status or upset others. Though they are able to find support from their community, it typically tends to be solution-based support, and often the root of the stress or the issue tends to be unaddressed because of the fear of what others in their community may think.[28]

Additionally, this overemphasis on what others think even defines one's sense of self. For example, in a collectivist culture, a person defines themselves relative to those in their community, with descriptions like, "I am a kind sibling; I'm a great spouse; I'm a giving caretaker," rather than recognizing traits like intellect, athleticism, or creativity.[29]

On the contrary, those growing up in individualistic cultures tend to define themselves by personal attributes, rather than focusing on their traits in relation to others. Thus, the individualistic citizen would use personality traits when describing themselves.[30] They also tend to have more transactional and revolving relationships, as their society allows for them to branch out and meet more people. Subsequently, they tend to have a greater sense of confidence in social interactions as they find the people who best fit their needs of a social circle. Some studies have been found that individualistic societies tend to have fewer societal norms that involve human touch, meaning fewer hugs and cheek kisses.[31]

Personally, I've found myself conflicted in defining who I am in relation to others and how they view me. It's that collectivist upbringing of wanting to be viewed as a great

---

28 Kendra Cherry, "Understanding Collectivist Cultures," Verywell Mind, Dotdash Publishing Family, reviewed on March 24, 2020.

29 Ibid.

30 Kendra Cherry, "Individualistic Cultures and Behavior," Verywell Mind, Dotdash Publishing Family, Reviewed on March 24, 2020.

31 Ava Rosenbaum, "Personal Space and American Individualism," Brown Political Review, Brown University, October 31, 2018.

friend, partner, and colleague, sometimes even more so than being known for my achievements. Yet no matter how much I try to get myself to slow down and focus on these relational goals, the drive of the individualistic culture in wanting to be unique forces me to overwhelm myself and keep going.

Ultimately, there is no objectively better culture, just one that may work better for others based on their purpose and view of life. But regardless, our environment affects us, and the difference in our community structures can make us feel lonely or insignificant. Without realizing it and understanding the effects of these two types of societies, it can feel like it's you against the world. But with proper knowledge and expectations, we can manage that mindset.

III.

STIGMA AND SURVIVAL

"I don't think you really have bipolar disorder."
"You can't tell people 'that'; they'll think you're crazy."
"Your symptoms aren't that bad. I don't think you really need medication."
"You just need to change your perspective and be more grateful. A lot of people have it so much worse."

Want to know one thing that all of the above quotes have in common? None of them were said by mental health experts or professionals. Despite that, hundreds of people I've interacted with in my life have uttered some variation of these opinions, disguised as facts, to me regarding my mental health. They couldn't believe someone who was able to manage their responsibilities could have the diagnosis of bipolar disorder. After all, for many, that label is often paired with other labels like "crazy," "homeless," and "uneducated."

The prejudice against mental illness is deep. Historically, people who were mentally ill would be locked up in asylums and have their humanity taken away from them. Even today, though society has made progress in accepting people who have a mental illness, negative prejudice and stigma orbit many diagnoses. This perception makes diagnoses feared, and people deny and fight them in ways that prevent them from getting the help they need. But is the stigma right?

"Natural selection could have eliminated anxiety, depression, addiction, anorexia and the genes that cause autism, schizophrenia and manic depressive illness. But it didn't. Why not?"
—RANDOLPH NESSE [32]

Speaking in evolutionary terms, Randolph Nesse brings up a good point. If mental illness was as bad as society believed it was, how and why would it be so prevalent in the human population? Our emotions have evolutionary purposes (i.e. to warn us against predators, or signal for us to treat a wound), and mental disorders are typically the by-product of experiencing an excess of these emotions. Evolution hasn't eliminated them through Darwinism because nature doesn't give a damn if we're happy; it simply wants us to survive.[33]

Our modern lives aren't as survival-driven as they were in the days of the cavemen. Therefore, excessive emotions may often prompt inappropriate responses that get in the way of social interaction. It may very well feel like our society has outgrown the need for these excessive emotions, but I would argue that it hasn't. This excess of emotions drives us to be more reactive and, in turn, think in ways that others aren't driven toward. We just need to find a way to manage it, and

---

32 Tim Adams, "Good Reasons for Bad Feelings Review – a New Approach to Mental Disorder," Review of *Good Reasons for Bad Feelings* by Randolph Nesse, *The Guardian*, March 17, 2019.

33 Ibid.

once we've got better control over it, we can channel it into amazing outcomes.

Once we view mental illness in a positive way, we can start taking steps to shift the negative view that the world has of mental illness. But to do that, we have to know what we're up against, and how it affects our process of healing. This negative obstacle, stigma, is the main thing that the concept of being "Outside of Your Head" fights to negate.

WHAT IS STIGMA?

The Oxford Dictionary defines stigma as "a mark of disgrace associated with a particular circumstance, quality, or person."[34] In the terms of mental illness, this mark of disgrace is associated with all three of the noted particularities. Stigma surrounds the *circumstances* of when negative symptoms flare up, the *qualities* that inconvenience others regarding someone's mental illness, and, after enough experience with the first two, the *person* themselves.

In other words, stigma is deeply rooted in every single aspect of the life of someone who lives with mental illness. Understanding stigma is important for both the sufferer and observer alike, to understand why its influence affects the healing process of mental illness as much as it does.

WHAT ARE COMMON STIGMAS REGARDING MENTAL ILLNESS?

I could name quite a few common stigmas simply based on what I've experienced. These disgraceful marks are like stickers on the person in question and they seem to travel through a crowd faster than an airborne virus.

---

34   *Oxford*, s.v. "stigma (_n._)," accessed April 30, 2020.

Dramatic. Lazy. Unreliable. Crazy.

Those are the main four that I've come across, but there are many more where that came from.

Violent. Dangerous. Unaware. Homeless. Ungrateful. Broken. Weak.

I could go on, but I'm sure that these are enough to paint a picture. The belief that mental illness is a choice, and that there's a fix to it, prompts a lot of this negativity. It can be very difficult for someone to truly be open about their mental state when they not only have to battle their symptoms, but also these terrible labels.

WHO HOLDS THESE STIGMAS?

The answer to this question is what can really make us feel like we're up against the world. That's because this answer is, in some capacity, every single one of us.

Even those of us who suffer from it, and deem ourselves to be the most understanding of mental illness in general, can hold these stigmas against people who suffer from other types of mental disorders. In a lot of ways, that's because we tend to be prejudiced against what we don't understand, and we can have a hard time understanding what we don't experience.

We see this unfold in many people in our lives, with the most problematic ones being those who hold positions of power over us. That could be our parents, teachers, legislators, or bosses. For example, a teenager who is suffering from depression cannot get care from a doctor unless it is discussed with their parents in the state of Florida. If their parents are worried that their child may be seen with these negative stigmas, they may downplay the symptoms their child exhibits and refrain from pursuing treatment. This scenario is just one example of how these views can drastically affect our acceptance of ourselves, access to resources, and, ultimately, the healing process.

HOW DO THEY AFFECT OUR HEALING?

The greatest chance we have to properly manage our mental illnesses presents itself in the early stages. If we're able to understand and manage our symptoms before they get out of hand, we can lead a life that minimizes the debilitating ways they can progress. The presence of these stigmas makes it difficult to do this.

When someone is surrounded by these negative stigmas, they can go into denial about having anything wrong with them; for fear of having those labels applied to them. They often start questioning whether or not they truly feel the ways that they do, and they begin to feel guilty. Thus, they don't seek out the help they need early on and can become trapped by the symptoms.

One example of a stigma that prominently affects the healing process is the one surrounding medications used to treat mental illness. I've heard them referred to as "crazy pills" that give people "fake happiness." I've also heard strong arguments against them that focus on the negative side effects that they bring.

Regardless of the complexities that are involved in the debate of these medications, they do serve a purpose and are very viable options for people who need help balancing their chemicals. But when subjected to all of these negative conversations, the people who take these pills begin to feel deficient for needing "fake happiness," or even "crazy" for their dependence on them. Often, these stigmas hurt their healing process, as people become less willing to look at these options.

On the other hand, no one makes someone taking medication treating a physical illness feel that way. Rather, they try to be supportive and provide reasonable access and accommodations for their medication. As a result, those people are more likely to stay on their medication, leading to better outcomes like quicker healing or fuller lives.

This is the difference that stigma can make.

HOW DO THEY AFFECT OUR DAILY LIVES?

These negative stigmas, when held by those people in positions of power who we mentioned, can affect our ability to be functioning members of society. When lawmakers hold negative stigmas, they can create laws regarding access to care and insurance funding that discriminate against mental illnesses. I know that on many of my health insurance plans, therapy funding, and even the selections of psychiatrists in-network, was never too great. This limitation has made it difficult for me to find convenient and quality care that could accommodate my work schedule and geographic location.

Additionally, employers can be less accommodating when they view mental illness negatively, causing them to not offer certain flexible working arrangements that are within their capabilities (like remote work or flexible work hours), which makes it hard for people to work around symptoms flaring up. This inflexibility not only hurts the person, as they have a harder time performing at their best, but also hurts the company that is missing out on the productivity and quality work this person can provide when they are fully supported.

In recent years, we're noticing (at least in the United States) a push for more sensitivity about and care for mental illness. More acceptance and education is being provided to the general public. But it wasn't always there, and that means many of us were affected by the negative stigma and misunderstandings growing up, so that is still a repercussion that some people are dealing with the fallout of.

WHAT CAN WE DO ABOUT IT?
This first step to changing something within the world is to change it within ourselves.

We are all guilty of having some sort of prejudice toward what we don't understand. By accepting this fault, we can pay attention to what our prejudices are and seek out education to help change them. Whether that happens through research, or by developing relationships with the people (or things) to which these stigmas are attached, it's our duty to try to understand. Then, through supporting and educating others with what we've learned, we can make progress toward creating communities that are more accepting of all sorts of different circumstances, qualities, and people.

Creating change really can be that simple.

IV.

SOON YOU'LL GET BETTER: THE TOOLS

―――

It's tiny, but it changes my entire world. It's round, and yet it makes me sharp. It calms me down enough to breathe, but also takes my breath away.

It's only one of many different tools I've used to get better.

It's my Risperidone pill. A dosage of half a milligram has the power to completely alter the way my mind approaches the day, with side effects that alter my breathing if I take them too soon before bed.

I've been on many medications for bipolar disorder. I've also tried natural supplements, therapy, exercise, and many other tools in managing my illness. Every single one was an important step on my journey with my mental illness, though I've found these tools have fluctuated in degrees of helpfulness throughout time. Before we can go into the cognitive reframing that this book focuses on, it's important to define what we focus on, and also discuss the methods used in managing mental illness.

WHAT IS MENTAL ILLNESS?

The American Psychiatric Association (APA) defines mental illness as health conditions involving changes in emotion, thinking, or behavior (or a combination of these). It also associates mental illnesses with distress and/or problems functioning in social, work, or family activities.[35]

When continuing your research on mental illness, you find it's a defined set of conditions within the medical world. This definition allows for insurance carriers to cover some of the costs associated with care, but it also means that mental illnesses are viewed as a condition that's treated through modern medicine. The latter is where the mindset of making it something we can "fix" is derived from.

HOW ARE THEY DEFINED?

This set of medical diagnoses is harbored in its respective mecca: The Diagnostic and Statistical Manual of Mental Disorders (DSM–5). The DSM-5 has taken over a decade to compile, and it serves as the authoritative volume on the definition, classification, and treatment of mental disorders.[36] The disorders covered in the DSM-5 are extensive, and it's a good place to get information on the medical practice regarding the treatment of mental disorders.

I'll define the following three diagnoses, since they will be the main focus in this book:

---

[35] Ranna Parekh, MD, "What Is Mental Illness?" American Psychiatric Association, American Psychiatric Association, August 2018.

[36] "DSM–5 Educational Resources," American Psychiatric Association, American Psychiatric Association, accessed May 3, 2020.

- Bipolar Disorder: "Bipolar disorders are brain disorders that cause changes in a person's mood, energy and ability to function. Bipolar disorder is a category that includes three different conditions—bipolar I, bipolar II and cyclothymic disorder. People with bipolar disorders have extreme and intense emotional states that occur at distinct times, called mood episodes. These mood episodes are categorized as manic, hypomanic or depressive. People with bipolar disorders generally have periods of normal mood as well."[37]
- Depression: "Depression (major depressive disorder) is a common and serious medical illness that negatively affects how you feel, the way you think and how you act. Depression causes feelings of sadness and/or a loss of interest in activities once enjoyed."[38]
- Anxiety: "Anxiety is a normal reaction to stress and can be beneficial in some situations. It can alert us to dangers and help us prepare and pay attention. Anxiety disorders differ from normal feelings of nervousness or anxiousness, and involve excessive fear or anxiety. Anxiety disorders are the most common of mental disorders and affect nearly 30 percent of adults at some point in their lives."[39]

---

37   Ranna Parekh, MD. "What Are Bipolar Disorders?" American Psychiatric Association, American Psychiatric Association, January 2017.

38   Ranna Parekh, MD. "What Is Depression?" American Psychiatric Association, American Psychiatric Association, January 2017.

39   Ranna Parekh, MD. "What Are Anxiety Disorders?" American Psychiatric Association, American Psychiatric Association, January 2017.

HOW CAN WE BREAK DOWN COPING METHODS?

One means of classifying coping methods into categories is in the dichotomy of problem-solving strategies and emotion-focused strategies. Problem-solving strategies are efforts to do something active to alleviate stressful circumstances, whereas emotion-focused strategies involve efforts to regulate the emotional consequences of stressful or potentially stressful events.[40]

Many of us deploy a mixture of the two based on our personal preference and each unique situation we're subjected to. In other words, everyone copes with the stressors in their life differently and on their own timeline. What works for me may not work for someone else, and vice versa, which means that if you're having a difficult time managing your symptoms, it may just mean you haven't found the right fit for you yet.

Dealing with a mental illness makes the stressors you have to cope with feel omnipresent, and it's a higher level of stimulation than those who are without a mental illness may be subjected to. A mental illness is like a roommate in your mind, and unlike one you share a living space with, you can't seem to escape this one. That's because escaping your mind isn't as easy as leaving your room.

Which brings us to another distinction in coping methods. These coping methods are the active approach and the avoidant approach. Their definitions can be assumed by their titles, but an active coping strategy focuses on responding in a way that will change either the stressor itself or your perspective on it. On the other hand, an avoidant coping

---

40   Shelley Taylor, "Coping Strategies," MacArthur | Research Network on SES & Health, University of California, San Francisco, July 1998.

strategy involves indulging in mental states or activities that keep you from addressing those stressors. The latter is linked to behaviors, such as alcoholism and withdrawal, that can be harmful for you once they get to that level.[41]

Let's think of this in terms of the roommate comparison.

Let's imagine that you're stuck in the apartment with your roommate 24/7 as a direct result of a pandemic-induced lockdown (which is the world's current reality as I write this chapter). You've spent your year with your roommate avoiding addressing issues like dishes, noise levels, laundry schedules, and now you're being forced to confront what you've let fester.

You may need some wine to deal with the stress and get your thoughts in order before you choose how you move forward with approaching this issue. Or you may need to go for a run, or avoid it for the night; all of which are okay.

But if you spend the next few months drinking away the stress and never addressing the built-up issues, they're never going to get better, and you're going to be subjected to the perpetual stress of an unhealthy living situation. All the while, you're subjecting your body to an overindulgence of the avoidance coping strategies that can be unhealthy.

Understanding your relationship with the tools you have for coping is the most important thing you can do for yourself in your journey of healing and lifetime management. You get to develop your own plan because you get to have that control of your life.

---

41 Shelley Taylor, "Coping Strategies," MacArthur | Research Network on SES & Health, University of California, San Francisco, July 1998.

WHAT ARE THE TOOLS WE CAN USE?

The traditional ways of treating mental illness, which are generally applied to all of the different disorders, are medications, therapy, brain-stimulation treatments, exercise, and diet. But your toolbox of treatments becomes more specific when your diagnosis, health, and preferences are taken into account.

Emotion-focused strategies can involve strategies that can help regulate emotions in the moment. Positive inner self-talk, crying, accepting the situation, venting, and screaming into a pillow are all examples of ways you allow yourself to express your emotions.

Problem-solving strategies can mean therapy, having an open conversation with the stressor, removing yourself from the situation, turning to support systems that can help you get out of your situation, and positive self-talk to reframe the way you perceive the issue.

Avoidant techniques could mean focusing on an object unrelated to the situation, drinking a glass of wine, denying the issue, or shutting down in the face of stress.

Active techniques could be doing something physical (like yoga), taking deep breaths during stressful periods, turning to faith-based practices and prayer, and taking medication.

You can put so many tools in your toolbox that it almost becomes a relief to know how much support you actually have. however, the abundance of tools can also be overwhelming.

HOW CAN I FIND WHICH TOOLS ARE RIGHT FOR ME?

You should ask yourself two questions when determining which tools might work for you:

1. What is the "why" behind your response to your stressor?
2. How do you feel when you use a tool in response to a stressor?

Finding out the "why" behind your response is important. If you look at issues on a surface level, you won't truly understand why you're feeling a certain way, and all your tools may feel ineffective. A very good application of answering this question is when I go into how I learned to manage my anger in a later chapter during the "Reflect" section. But if a stressor makes you behave a certain way that others deem inappropriate, evaluate the triggers from your life that could possibly be evoking your emotional response.

Evaluating how you feel when using a tool is important because nothing will ever improve without thoughtful consideration and feedback. We may not know what's right, but we do know what feels right. If you're working out and something hurts, you should stop and revaluate your form. The same concept applies here.

WHY DO TOOLS THAT USED TO WORK STOP FEELING RIGHT?

Throughout your life, your needs will change, just as your symptoms will. With different symptoms, different life experiences, and different triggers, your tool box and personal regiment of managing your symptoms will need to adapt.

This change is why the second question of "how do you feel?" is so important. As you pay attention and notice that it hurts, it's ineffective, or it feels off, you can give yourself a break. These "transitionary" stages of readjusting our self-care regiment are a part of life, and they can be fun, creative, and exciting. We can look at it as a new adventure or a different path, rather than a burden.

Just as we must realign our skills and schedules to cater to our daily duties, we also must realign our coping mechanisms to deal with what we're suffering through. But knowing our needs will change and these "transitionary" periods will occur doesn't mean it's going to be easy when they do.

Sometimes, certain tools are difficult to use because solving problems and experiencing growth can be hard. The tool of therapy may make you unpack some difficult unresolved feelings, just like the tool of medication may make you experience a funk or some side effects until you and your doctor find the right medication and dosage. Knowing that it's going to be uncomfortable may seem acceptable if you're feeling alright, but when your symptoms make you feel awful, it can be hard to find the motivation to apply the tools that aren't a quick fix.

WHAT'S THE MOST IMPORTANT THING ON THE JOURNEY OF HEALING?

You need to know *you deserve it*, and *want to get better*.

I know that I deserve the right to feel okay, that I deserve to work on myself and apply tools, and I want to get better, be better, and feel better. Yet I still find myself slipping, and it gets really hard at times. Sometimes I succeed, and sometimes I fail, but it's all part of the journey.

Often, we tell ourselves our symptoms aren't "as bad" as someone else's, and we allow stigma or the fear of failure to make us afraid. But the biggest thing you need to learn for you and everyone around you is this: you'll never benefit from help until you accept that you want it and you need it. Letting it fester can cause your condition to become extremely difficult to manage, and it can hurt you and the people around you more than you could have imagined.

WILL I EVER GET BETTER?

Yes. You do every day. You reflect, you learn, you become more aware with yourself, and you maintain some type of dedication to something you love that can serve as your motivation. All of us want to get better. Any type of recovery is a journey, with relapses, disappointments, mistakes, and heartache for all involved, but that's a smaller portion of the journey in comparison to the successes, wins, and celebratory moments of growth.

In your conversations with yourself and loved ones who suffer with mental illness, provide support, love them, and remind them of what they love. The conversations should be motivational, revolve around why they want to feel better, and provide support even when they falter.

The hard part about reflection and the tools you utilize is that they take effort to enforce. When you're in your lowest moments, it can feel impossible to grasp onto them and use them. So just remind yourself of why you want it, and do the best you can every day.

A CONNECTION (WITH ME)

It was a beautiful Saturday morning. I spent Friday night in and, through a burst of productivity, completed some tasks with looming deadlines that were taunting me. I got to wake up next to my favorite little pup in the world, Daisey, and met my best friend for one of our infamous boxing workout classes. All smiles, we moved the party over to our favorite coffee shop, and in the midst of sipping my matcha latte, I felt it.

I instantly lost my ability to focus on the conversation.

My eyes felt dry.

I felt like the only motivation I had was to get into bed and curl up into a ball…and the only way to relieve the dry pain in my eyes was to cry them to sleep.

I never really know when it's going to hit, but when it does, it's inescapable.

You can do everything right, surround yourself with the people whom you love, and celebrate your successes, but the emptiness that comes with depression is an ocean that washes over you and makes you drown.

Growing up, I struggled with it, and its symptoms pervaded into my existence at an extremely early age. My first memories of senselessly crying myself to sleep at night came when I was about ten years old. Very young, very impressionable, and very desperate to understand this illness, I spent years trying to figure out the "cure" that society kept telling me was out there.

I tried it all: medication, counseling, therapy, support from loved ones, exercise, natural supplements, but none of it yielded this elusive "fix." The journey of trying to find it was daunting, and exhausting, and it led me to fall further into my depression. I took my failure personally, and I felt inadequate and broken in my inability to find this damn "cure."

I took it upon myself to overcompensate for that failure by turning into a workaholic, and succumbing to other similar vices. I couldn't depend upon myself to feel good, but I could depend upon my ability to work harder than others around me. Thus, I achieved a lot of traditional successes academically and professionally, while also investing into experiences like volunteering and traveling that momentarily felt enriching. But they failed to fill the emptiness I knew I had inside. Even when I was celebrating, I often felt the dark cloud and the anxiety of losing everything looming over me.

These methods of overcompensation not only failed to add meaning to the persistent emptiness I felt, but also began to contradict and invalidate my feelings to the people in my life. As I fell into these depressions, my friends and family would use these achievements as a basis to tell me that I didn't have any "reason" to be depressed. They would say that I needed to "change my attitude" and understand how "blessed" or "grateful" I should feel.

Well, their advice was only further making me feel like a failure for failing to fix the hardest and most defining obstacle in my life. As a result, I disassociated from everyone and hid my feelings with shame. Until finally, one day, it hit me.

There is no "cure" as we traditionally define it, and I finally accepted I would never truly be able to change this about myself…because my mental illness was a part of me, and it still is. It defines the way that I think, and it's given me strength and resilience through making me fight it all my life. I realized that, though difficult, it taught me lessons and made me a more determined person.

Finally, I stopped feeling broken. I recognized that I was just different, "weird" as some may say, and that is okay.

For many of us who suffer from chronic and diagnosed mental disorders like depression, anxiety, or bipolar disorders, among many others, the symptoms can be debilitating. And like the common cold, we're just looking for the best syrup that can mask the pain to make us feel like we can go tackle the rest of our days.

In the world of mental illness, medicine, exercise, supplements, and support systems are all of that: they are very helpful and necessary tools that we can use to alleviate the burden of the symptoms. But the one thing they don't do is "fix" the illness. They do, however, give you an outlet for those excess emotions that mental illness tends to induce.

We are not independent of our illnesses. We are intertwined with them in our strands of DNA. By allowing society to make us believe that mental illness can be fixed, we fail to accept the disposition that will never truly leave us, even if we allow it to manifest into different means.

My mental disposition has evolved greatly over the thirteen years I've been struggling with it. But the greatest change has come in the way that I view it: it is a part of me, and it makes me different, but different isn't always a bad thing. It sometimes sucks. I go to the gym every day, I practice yoga and meditation, I have a dog who provides emotional support, and much more. But if I fall out of a routine, or become overwhelmed with stress, it is vulnerable to falling apart.

I know this reality now, and I accept it and plan for it the best I can. I make workout plans with friends to hold myself accountable, I talk to my therapist weekly, and when I do fall apart, I don't beat myself up over it. My life and journey now are focused on managing my symptoms, not trying to cure them. This shift in mindset has alleviated a lot of weight off of my shoulders.

My symptoms already make me feel like shit; I don't need the journey of healing to make me feel that way, too.

If I focus so much on thinking that the steps I take to manage my symptoms are supposed to cure them, then I get discouraged and stop taking those steps. Rather than being grateful for the progress in my mental health they support, I shame them and give up on them for not curing me.

My journey of acceptance has allowed me to better manage my life. I am no longer burdened by the tireless search for a solution that doesn't exist. And by accepting this part of me, I've been able to use it and see the silver lining in the lessons and skills that it's taught me.

The culmination of over a decade of my struggles prompted me to organize them into steps. When I broke it down, I realized that there were three main phases of getting myself to a healthier place:

1. Accepting: The first part of my journey was accepting small truths that allowed me to fixate less on situations that used to trigger my depressive episodes.
2. Reflecting: After accepting lessons that helped me understand where I should focus my energy, I spent a lot of time reflecting on some of the "why" and "what" of different themes that influenced me and my mental illness. This provided greater and more in-depth lessons that helped me better understand myself, as well as the small truths.
3. Embracing: The part of my journey where I began to see the benefits in the skills and mindsets my journey allowed me to adopt, and embracing it in a way that's led me to greater success.

I don't have all the answers, and I will be the first to admit that I'm not perfect. But I believe the things that have helped me can help others too. This book takes you through my journey and hopefully shares my lessons for you in yours. Whether you're reading this book to better understand yourself or a loved one who suffers with managing their disorder, welcome. We've got quite a journey ahead of us.

ACCEPT

I.
'ACCEPT' INTRODUCTION

"I didn't know it was a problem, until...."

Finish that sentence. If it seems hard to do at first, think of a time when you uttered these words in an effort to explain an action you may have not been proud of.

I can give a precedent of this regarding my control issues. "I didn't know it [my control issues] was a problem, until" I found out my best friend was going out of her way to plan me a thoughtful and elaborate surprise birthday party a few days before it was set to take place. My hypervigilant persona dug too deep and I found out what she was doing, ruining both her spirits in an effort to do a kind deed for me and the potential elated feeling I would've had from the surprise.

For any of us who have gone through any kind of therapy or reformative counseling, we've probably heard this saying before: acceptance is the first step on the road toward healing. Unlike some utter fallacies that we may be subjected to over and over again, this one has a lot of merit to it. This section of our book is focused on the concept of acceptance.

Each of the following chapters is a lesson I've learned accompanied by the anecdotes that caused me to finally accept it. Though I had a lot of ideas for which lessons to include, I picked the ones ahead because of not only their connection with my mental illness, but also their impact on a large number of people I met. A lot have to do with expectations, loss, sacrifices, and interpersonal relationships. Typically, these events have provided opportunities that have exacerbated my symptoms. Thus, these lessons were the ones I thought were most important in helping me not take things so personally, and ultimately made these instances affect me a little less.

By discussing the moments of accepting our troubles and recognizing the challenges we may face, we can lead ourselves into the reflections that make our experiences lessons rather than transactions.

II.

THE WORLD DOESN'T REVOLVE AROUND ME

―

Experiences from your childhood are more than just memories. Often, they are blueprints to who you are as an adult.

For the first ten years of my life, I was the baby in my family. During that time, it felt as if the whole world revolved around me. Being quite academically inclined, I had a lot of achievements that made me feel like a pretty special kid. I won a Pride Award in math, I had been tested and marked gifted due to my IQ in the third grade, and I even got a Citizen's award twice for being the best "citizen" in my school in both kindergarten and fourth grade. It was hard not to feel special.

Many of us often build our identities, especially in these formative years, on how others perceive us. If we're in a constant state of being awarded for our achievements, we begin to form a worldview of entitlement that often follows us into adulthood.

Though I never truly believed that the world revolved around me (I was, after all, academically inclined enough to understand the way the solar system operated), I felt like I could get special treatment. This mindset followed me into the late stages of my adolescence and caused me a great deal of disappointment when that wasn't the case. Accepting that the world didn't revolve around me was important, but it was a journey of taking pills that were hard to swallow. Despite how much special treatment I may have felt, I began taking these pills early on in those formative elementary school years.

I was awarded the part of a solo to sing in one of our musical numbers for the school's Christmas concert. Unfortunately, my parents were unable to provide transportation (because of their work schedules) for me to attend a significant number of rehearsals leading up to the concert. I practiced at home by myself and felt confident that I was talented enough to deliver my performance. However, about a week before the show, I went into music class and my teacher pulled me aside.

"You've missed a lot of rehearsals, and I've made the decision to give your solo to another girl who's attended all of the rehearsals," she regretfully informed me. I would not have an opportunity to sing individually.

Being ten, I was devastated. I felt like someone with the privilege of having parents who worked flexible hours was being given something that I was more qualified for simply because my parents worked odd hours in manufacturing and couldn't provide me with a ride to rehearsals. I lost any desire to show up for the performance, and my mom's sadness at the loss of my solo only fueled this feeling.

It all felt so unfair. During the next week's "creative hour" (this was an hour on a Friday during which we were allowed to go to either art or music class, but we were required to inform our teachers of our choice ahead of time), I decided to stray from my scheduled music session to go to art class instead. In art, I felt special. I was praised for my work and I wasn't being halted from showcasing my talent because of something I couldn't control. But there was a structure in having to inform your teachers of your whereabouts, and I disobeyed it.

When I returned to class after my art lesson, my primary teacher pulled me aside and explained the issue with directly disobeying a procedure.

"We have these rules in place for your safety. It's super dangerous and scary if I don't know where you are, and I'm going to assume the worst if you don't show up to the class you were supposed to," she said. "I could write you a disciplinary referral for this that's going to go your permanent record."

I was so embarrassed, and I finally admitted to her that I was too ashamed of my shortcomings with the music situation to approach her and rearrange what I would do for my creative hour. She spared me the referral, but she did make me talk to my music teacher and address the issue. My music teacher stood firm on her stance with the solo, and I had to partake in the concert as a member of the chorus. This instance was the first time I experienced the lack of special treatment that knocked me off my pedestal.

It can be really difficult for any of us to accept being punished for circumstances outside of our control, especially if we're doing everything in our power to ensure that we're deserving of what we've had taken away from us. In this instance, I still put in the work to practice and learn my solo, just not in the presence of my music teacher.

I was too young to let this incident offset all of the special treatment my other achievements and status had earned me up until that point, so I battled with the lesson of accepting that the world didn't revolve around me.

"If I can do enough things to prove I'm special, then people will have to treat me like I am," I used to naively tell myself.

As the universe does, it sent me many reinforcements for the lesson I had been shown during my solo experience. Sometimes, these reinforcements were in the form of late fees on payments or zeros on assignments I couldn't turn in on time because of circumstances that were similar in nature to the one for losing my solo. But they still weren't enough to truly teach me this lesson. Until my senior year of high school, that is.

During my final year, with the goal of graduating high school early, I took a few extra courses online during my second-to-last semester to fulfill the requirements for graduation. Because of the overwhelming workload of AP classes, volunteering, officer positions in organizations, and other life-related reasons, I didn't finish one of those classes until the first week of the following semester. The teacher of this course took no issue with extending my timeline, and my grade was unaffected.

I thought all was well and my excitement to graduate and begin college was higher than ever. But then, as an editor in the yearbook, I got a peak into the "Top 10" page before it was sent off to print. This "Top 10" page commemorated the prestigious group of seniors with the ten highest GPAs in their graduating class. These people were rewarded with a small scholarship, a special feature in the graduation ceremony, and a celebratory dinner with the principal and administration of the school.

Based on my GPA, I was qualified for seventh place. But when I looked at the page, I noticed there was another face and name in that spot. I immediately asked my yearbook teacher if I could have a hall pass to go see my guidance counselor, which she granted, and within ten minutes I was sitting in front of my guidance counselor hoping she could tell me this was a mistake.

"Let me check your file," she said. I watched her input some information onto her computer, and after a minute, she looked at me conclusively. "It looks like you completed your online economics course two days after the start of this semester. That means you had 20.5 credit hours when we counted GPAs, which was the day before the semester started, and you needed 21 credit hours to be considered."

I was flustered. "But I finished that course only two days later. The announcements aren't even finalized. I just know because of the yearbook proof we haven't sent to print yet. And no one told me that this would be a consequence when I asked for an extension on my class."

"Unfortunately, there's nothing I can do about it. These are the rules."

I paused for a moment, and then I responded the only thing I could at the moment: "I understand."

I got up from the chair and left the office feeling defeated.

On numerous occasions, many of us have thought that we've covered all our bases, just to be told that, in our research, no one informed us of something that is now affecting our ability to succeed at the task at hand. This moment was one of those instances when I thought that I had done everything right, only to hear what too many of us have heard in our lives: nothing can be done about it. Even if that truly is the case, it doesn't make it any less devastating or devaluating when you're the recipient of that line.

Looking back, I recognize how little that status meant. My GPA spoke for itself when it needed to during college admissions and scholarship decisions. But for someone who had sacrificed so much and truly only ever felt that uniqueness or special treatment in her academic achievements, I was beyond devastated. Mistakes and mishaps occur, but the fact that they were so unwilling to do anything about it to mediate the problem with me was the worst part. I felt so worthless, and so insignificant in the world.

But I was awarded a distraction in the form of good news a few weeks later that overshadowed the unfortunate "Top 10" disappointment: my partner and I won first place in states in our Future Business Leaders of America (FBLA) competition, and our district would fully sponsor our trip to go to Nationals and compete on behalf of our school.

I hadn't been on a plane since my family immigrated from Serbia. We were working class, so the only vacation I had ever gotten during my childhood was an overnight stay in Miami when I was thirteen that was the result of my mom having a meltdown over working so much and never being able to afford a vacation. The trip to Nationals was an amazing opportunity, and it felt like my luck was turning around.

However, the world does not revolve around me, and it had different plans for how that year was going to play out.

In registering for summer classes to initiate my first semester of college, I found out that the dates of the first week conflicted with my Nationals trip. Immediately, I searched the internet and found the number of the advisor for my academic department. I called him, and explained the situation.

"Congratulations on that awesome opportunity. If you don't attend your first day, you will lose your spot in the class, and if it fills up, you may not be able to take it until the following semester. I see that since it's a prerequisite to your calculus class in the fall, it could mess up your schedule, and your scholarship for dropping below your stated enrollment status. But if you get your professor's permission beforehand, they can avoid marking you "absent" and you can go to your competition while keeping your seat," he explained.

"I'm drafting an email already," I joked.

I sent those emails within ten minutes of the end of that phone call and followed up at least three times. One of the professors gave me permission, but another one wouldn't respond to his email or to the voicemails I left on his office phone. As a result, I had to lose out on being able to compete in Nationals in favor of doing college pre-calculus at the university library (I'm still trying to figure out what that was karma for).

That instance finally made me accept I wasn't inherently special or deserving of any special treatment, and I couldn't expect the world to make exceptions for me, even though it may be warranted. No matter how hard I worked, the world still had an order, and there were consequences and reactions to going against the flow of things. But in many ways, it brought a sense of relief, similar to the relief I felt in the realization I brought up in the "Introduction" and "Background" sections of realizing there wasn't a "cure" for my mental illness.

A lot of my depressive episodes, and many painful memories, were triggered by instances like these when I had an expectation, or some feeling of entitlement (whether valid or not), that wasn't met. Not meeting these expectations prompted feelings of failure that made it more difficult for me to process the natural disappointment that happens when things don't go your way. Disappointment is natural and a part of the human experience, but controlling our expectations can help us mitigate the negative effects of it.

What I learned when I finally accepted that I wasn't intrinsically special or "at the center of the universe" was that knowing that was a relief. Trying to maintain an image that was shrouded in overachievement was exhausting, and it was always causing me to put more stuff on my plate. Having had such high academic marks and achievements made it really difficult for me to swallow any shortcomings. It also made it hard to enjoy the successes because my mind was always on the future, and never in the present.

Not being officially celebrated as the Top 10 in my high school class was difficult for me because the identity I created for myself was intertwined with being academically "special." But the timing of my partner's and my state win in our FBLA competition came shortly after this news, and it reminded me that there are so many opportunities out there and that you can make yourself into who you want to be. You just can't focus your identity on one thing.

I came to realize that my self-identity was fluid, and I could shape it by the kind of person I was, rather than being so reliant on the need to feel special and at the center of the universe. Besides, accepting that I wasn't uniquely special helped me stop focusing so much on myself, and pushed me to pay more attention to the people in my life. After all, they're the only ones who can truly make you feel special.

III.

YOU'RE NEVER GOING TO BE 'THE BEST': RELATIONSHIPS WITH FAILURE

From what you've read about me so far, I'm sure it's easy to imagine how hard this lesson was for me to accept in my young life. I always wanted to be the best at whatever I did, sometimes sacrificing my sleep and my health to achieve some arbitrary goal I thought would make me special or unique. In a society that seemingly defines us by our accomplishments, job titles, and net worth, this desire may read familiar to many of you who are reading this chapter.

But as your network and exposure to multiple expectations builds through life, and competition and standards of beauty, success, and productivity have increased, arguably, beyond what someone can naturally achieve, clinging to this desire can be extremely harmful for your mental health. Defining your worth by comparison to others is ultimately unsustainable because there's always someone who'll come along and be better than you at what you thought you had mastered. At the end of the day, you just have to accept this fact and know that it doesn't mean that your life is any less meaningful.

If I was given a dime for every time I read a headline in my life titled "record-breaking," I'd be writing this book from the beaches of Fiji rather than my bedroom. The abundance of records broken on a consistent basis is astounding, and they show how an achievement that someone spends a lifetime becoming "the best" at can quickly be overshadowed by someone better.

If you define your identity and value by this title of being "the best," inevitably being stripped of it or realizing it's unattainable will shatter your world. Thus, accepting that attempting to be the best at everything is not only impossible, but also a counterproductive state of mind early on is important for a healthy state of mind.

Here are a few things that come with accepting that you'll never truly be "the best" at something:

1. Adjectives like "the best" are relative. The relativity is most typically to your competition, or to the criteria by which you're being judged. Neither of these will ever be exhaustive, or undeniably objective, so the concept of "the best" is constructed.
2. Experience is subjective. Relating back to the chapter on the introduction to the brain, we know that though there are biological connections to everything we feel and experience, we truly do not understand the brain in a way that makes us able to quantify the experience of living. As a result, our experiences are subjective, and

all of our realities are unique to us. Now, experience is a teacher, and it is also a building block to our values, so our experiences shape what we perceive to be "the best," and shape how we choose it.
3. Opinions are personal. This idea builds off all our experiences being unique to us. Since awards are the basis of subjective criteria and opinions, what we perceive to be "the best" of something will never be passed by acclamation.

These realizations tie into the lesson in the previous chapter that I'm not particularly special or at the center of the universe. The entitlement and perspective that stem from believing you are the best at something fuels the idea that you believe you deserve special treatment, which we learned isn't the case in our world. However, before I accepted that I'll never be the best at something, I really did a number on my mental health by beating myself up over trying to be the best.

Back to the nature vs. nurture argument: there is predisposition and ability defined in you when you're born. You can train to realize or even push those natural limits, but you have to accept who you are and know that part of the equation will never be changed. For example, Michael Phelps is known in pop culture as one of the best, if not the best, swimmers in the world. This renown is in large part due to his incredible training regimen, dedication, and mental dexterity in overcoming all his fears, insecurities, and challenges on his path to the Olympic sweep.

I also read articles as a kid after his Olympic medal sweep that his torso shape and other physiological features make him an amazing swimmer, in addition to all of his training and hard work. I could train twice as hard as Michael Phelps for twice as long, and only be a fraction of the swimmer he is because my body is designed very differently from his body. I could greatly improve and become a competent swimmer, but my body is cursed with a predisposition to be negatively buoyant (I even opened up this book with a story of me almost drowning in non-combative water). I could work as hard as possible and at the end of the day, I will never be on the level of Michael Phelps.

But, for as good as he is, there could be someone with a stronger and faster swimming ability than his. The only thing that's keeping them from taking that title of being "the best" competitive swimmer from Phelps is an opportunity.

However, we never see it that way, especially when we're at the top. For me, it was always academically, and in some sense, career-wise. I was universally known as a student who was good at everything. So anytime someone scored higher than me on a test or in a class, I felt like my title, and my entire perception of my self-worth, was at risk, and it scared me. What I know now is that it wasn't even a true title to begin with, because there is always someone better than you, and that has been a liberating realization.

Think of the NFL draft. Every single player in the draft was "the best of the best" at their respective schools. But when they get elevated to selections for the next level, they, all of a sudden, have much more competition. If they based their identities, self-worth, and futures on being a professional football player, which most of them do, the heartbreak and shock that come from not being selected are devastating, especially since many of them have worked countless hours and dedicated their entire lives to this goal.

Likewise, college freshmen who enter Ivy League institutions often face major shock when they transition from being the brightest mind at their high school to just another student in a brilliant school of fish. They were a big fish in a small pond, but now they're a comparatively smaller fish in a deep sea. As we've seen in previous chapters, feeling small in a sea prompts the potential for an overwhelming depression, especially if your entire identity and self-worth were built upon being the biggest fish.

But if in both situations the people could accept that there are better players, better students, better anything than what they've built their identities on, they stop focusing on this arbitrary title, and they have an opportunity to see their experiences and hard work as a means for personal growth, rather than a title.

Just because you've lost the self-constructed illusion of being "the best" doesn't mean it's all been a waste. You broke personal records, you learned new knowledge, you strengthened your body and mind, you made connections and friendships, and you pushed yourself to be the best version of you. You allowed your passions to be focused on bettering yourself and meeting your goals, which, as we mentioned in the "Soon You'll Get Better" chapter, is the most important mindset in enriching your life journey of mental well-being.

Just because you aren't "the best" in your new setting doesn't invalidate everything you did up until that point, and it doesn't redefine you as a failure; it simply presents a new chapter, lesson, or challenge.

If the students didn't go to their Ivy League institutions, they would miss out on the opportunity to enrich themselves from the valuable knowledge and connections that only a select few get to benefit from. If the NFL draft picks never tried, even if they didn't make it onto a team, they would forever miss out on an opportunity to get name recognition during the process and closure on that chapter of their life. Similarly, if you quit an opportunity because you get overwhelmed by the competition, you'll never know what good it could have brought you.

I've failed numerous times, and I've been just another small fish in a big sea. I applied for law school in my final year of undergrad and never got a response from my chosen university. I injured myself to the point of not being able to compete during my first and only high school track season. I bit off more than I could chew in terms of voluntary responsibilities, and I was not a great worker or leader to any of the organizations because I stretched myself so thin. I was not only not "the best," but I was also not even good in a lot of these situations. But I don't regret any of these failures, because I learned from them. If you always need to be "the best" at something to do it, you'll miss out on finding what activities and components build your personal reality of an authentic and happy life.

Not letting these failures define me is what helped me recognize the takeaway from each experience, whether that be a better understanding of work-life balance, which physical fitness activities my body was better built for, or what career choices were ultimately better for me and the lifestyle I wanted to live.

I strived for perfection, and when I didn't achieve it, I punished myself for it. I let myself invalidate any talent I had because of it. I stopped doing things I loved and I hurt myself because I allowed failures and challenges to weigh me down in my journey through life. But I've seen so many loved ones do the same thing, and ultimately miss out on opportunities due to their fear of failure and inability to live up to the faulted construct of being "the best."

But by accepting that no one will ever truly achieve this title, that there will always be someone better, and that perfection is not the goal, we have the freedom to choose our goals for ourselves, and actually succeed at them. It's incredible how much better you become when the focus is self-improvement rather than some arbitrary title.

IV.

SOMETIMES, YOU HAVE BAD TIMING

It's a Friday night. You're at your local comedy club sitting at a table, chatting up your group, and enjoying the food and beverages you're indulging in as you wait for the set to begin. You're excited! It's been a long week, but with good friends and stronger-than-average cocktails, you're ready to laugh away all of the stress you've endured.

The comedian comes on, and he makes a joke about the food. He picks a guy out from the crowd wearing a funny hat. He comically hits on a girl with a boyfriend sitting next to her. It's all being done so well, and everything is going great.

Then, he sets up a joke you're ready to spit your whiskey out at…and crashes it into the Hudson River.

God, what a bummer. He had everything right, with a level of momentum that was envious. But then, he ruined it all with his bad timing.

The mood changes, and all of sudden, everything you had hoped to get rid of comes rushing back. Unsure of your likeliness to return, you sulk through the rest of the set, and go home. All of this because of a little bad timing.

Whenever I'm asked for an example of bad timing in my life, I think about my family's arrival into a New York City airport shortly after 9/11 took place. Security was, understandably, on edge. They confiscated my brother's toy gun from his checked bag, and they were strict about us staying in our seats for the duration of the very long plane ride. In addition to those minor inconveniences, people weren't very welcoming toward us during those initial days because of our inability to speak the English language.

The paranoia it instilled in me made me paranoid of flying for a long time. But after conditioning myself with hundreds of safe flights over the years, I realized my paranoia was the result of bad timing that my brain mentally associated with the experience I had as an impressionable child.

We've discussed the importance of accepting we'll never be "the best" and touched on the concept of reevaluating our worth in the face of failure. Accepting that sometimes our failures are the result of external forces that are inevitable, can help us not be so hard on ourselves.

I've personally punished myself for not being enough. I've focused on failed relationships, friendships, and endeavors, and blamed myself to an unhealthy degree, even when other factors like timing, distance, or market volatility deserved a bigger slice of the blame cake.

My current state is being at home in quarantine. The COVID-19 pandemic has shut everything down. Businesses are failing, retirement accounts and life savings are depleting, students are graduating and unable to find jobs, and people with careers they've spent their entire lives working toward are applying for unemployment, with no guarantee of when they'll be able to return to normal.

People can argue all they want about whether or not the people who've been affected had proper risk management. They can state that someone should have had more savings, should have put their retirement account into less "risky" investments, or studied or worked toward "essential" jobs. But these arguments are futile because this situation is just an extreme case of really bad timing. And as the pandemic has come to show us, bad timing affects everyone.

Whether you believe it or not, the fact is this: timing is everything. An amazing joke can become a dud if you tell it at the wrong time, a cake recipe can become Chernobyl if your cooking time is off, and the love of your life can become your greatest "what if" if you lose them because you're not ready.

I once worked with two separate female coworkers who were married to men they had originally dated when they were younger but pushed away during a time when they weren't able to invest in the relationship the way they needed to for it to flourish. Both of them told me that their now-husbands had taken it hard, and both parties had spent their years apart with other people. But nothing ever felt the same way because no one was as right for them as they were for each other. They simply had bad timing in their youth, and recognizing that for themselves is what helped them accept another chance with each other when the timing was right.

Though the concept of "bad timing" is typically associated with love, it can also be applied in many different scenarios.

A few years ago, I wanted a dog more than anything. I was going through a rough time emotionally, and I really needed the support that a furry companion could bring. I found a senior dog (age thirteen) on the Internet who I fell in love with before I even met her. But before I could get her, I found out she passed away. Devastated, I halted my dog search for a year.

Once I couldn't hold out any longer, I started looking for another dog. I found one on Craigslist being re-homed by owners who were older and had just found out that one of them had a serious heart condition. I, again, fell in love with the photo of the dog and wanted to meet her. After getting in contact with the owners, they started pushing me away, and I felt as if I'd never get the dog. In a last attempt, I went to a shelter, fell in love with another dog, but before I could adopt her, some other family took her away.

At this point, I'd given up on the dog, and focused on getting a new job. Right when I started my new job, which involved long days of training, and I had a weeklong cruise planned within two weeks, I got contacted by the owners of the dog I found on Craigslist asking me if I still wanted to adopt her. This is the story of how I got Daisey.

But that first month of trying to train my new puppy Daisey, I was barely around, and it caused me to lose a pair of Armani glasses, an Xbox controller, and my sanity. I still adore her and am happy I went through with it, but that was just some crappy timing.

But had I not gone through with the timing, I would have missed out on my favorite little creature in the world, just as if my former coworkers hadn't accepted the role of bad timing in the dissolution of their former relationships, they may have ruined them by forcing themselves to stay in them, or not accepting another chance when it presented itself.

External forces have the ability to come in and completely unravel the intricate network you've built in your life. It can displace you physically, mentally, and financially, all in the passing of a second. If it's not a pandemic, it can be a hurricane, a tornado, a recession, automation, or the death of loved ones.

Accepting that sometimes we have bad timing is important for us to know when things don't work out. So many things threaten our way of life, and yet we don't cease to live. That doesn't mean you stop planning, or blame yourself: you simply learn to adjust to whatever new normal you must face. It may be bad timing, but just because it's not happening now doesn't mean it never will.

And for every bit of bad timing, there is timing that lands at just the right moment, but you're not going to reap the benefits if you're glooming over a poorly delivered joke.

V.

PEOPLE HAVE RIGHTS, AND YES, IT'S INCONVENIENT

Rights are inconvenient. If they weren't, history wouldn't have a track record of making them something people have died fighting for.

"Injustice anywhere is a threat to justice everywhere."
—DR. MARTIN LUTHER KING, JR. [42]

Though our society has recognized a set of universal human rights, many people are still fighting the battles of injustices against these rights every day. Our support of them in their victory is important, because, as Dr. King said, an injustice (and intolerance) against someone's

---

42   Dr. Martin Luther King Jr. *Quotations of Martin Luther King Jr.* (Carlisle, MA: Applewood Books, 2004), 13.

well-being in one area of the world can ripple into the rest of it.

Often, these injustices may seem so far away from us that, out of convenience and self-interest, we pay them minimal attention. But that's because it's hard for us to register the impact of an injustice until it happens to us or a loved one.

Now, fighting the war against human rights violations is something many of us will only donate to charities for rather than fight ourselves, but we can practice the act of respect for the rights of ourselves and others in our lives so that we keep an injustice from trickling into the lives of others.

Which brings me to a very important lesson I've learned: people have a right to their feelings, and yes, sometimes, it's an inconvenience. A human's right to their feelings is **not** on the same scope of the human rights fights that many individuals continue to fight and die over to simply stay alive, but they can be intertwined.

Two articles of the Universal Declaration of Human Rights (UDHR) that come to mind as constantly seeing this overlap are the following:

Article twelve.

No one shall be subjected to arbitrary interference with his privacy, family, home or correspondence, nor to attacks upon his honour and reputation. Everyone has the right to the protection of the law against such interference or attacks.⁴³

Article twenty-five.

(1) Everyone has the right to a standard of living adequate for the health and well-being of himself and of his family, including food, clothing, housing and medical care and necessary social services, and the right to security in the event of unemployment, sickness, disability, widowhood, old age or other lack of livelihood in circumstances beyond his control."⁴⁴

One's interpretation of what they deem as an interference or attack from Article twelve, as well as what they deem is the standard of living that will help them maintain their well-being mentally from Article twenty-five, is subject to their feelings. In both cases, rights are valued, protected, and not always convenient to all parties involved.

A lot of memories come to mind when I think of this lesson. One of them is from a solo trip I took to Barcelona a few years back. The beauty of solo travel is the peace of being with yourself for an extended period of time. Traveling alone can be very daunting, though, especially when it comes to speaking the local language. I have a relatively good grasp

---

43 "Universal Declaration of Human Rights," United Nations: Peace, dignity and equality on a healthy planet, United Nations, accessed on May 16, 2020.

44 Ibid.

of the Spanish language, and I'm able to communicate well enough to get myself where I need to be. Barcelona is a part of the Catalonia region, but most of its citizens are bilingual in both Spanish and Catalan.

In October 2017, Catalonia had written up a referendum claiming its independence from Spain, but the international community did not recognize its legitimacy. When I arrived in December, they were still a part of Spain, and the wound and distaste the citizens had from this fact was unavoidable. I was first subjected to it at the train station right outside the airport. I was having a hard time understanding how to purchase a ticket on the (literally) foreign kiosk.

I looked to the employee in uniform and asked, "¿Puedes ayudarme?" (Can you help me?)

He gave me a disgusted look and began to respond in the Catalan language. Despite seeing that I was not from the area, and while being on duty with the purpose of assisting travelers with questions, this man decided to make his dissatisfaction with the current state of affairs very known to me. He refused to speak to me in any Spanish, and, ultimately, I had to keep playing with the machine until I got a ticket that Google Maps said would take me to my hostel. On the train, I couldn't help but think what an ass that guy was.

But when I mellowed out, my view of him was more empathetic. He was passionate about something, and he was completely invalidated by it from the international community, of which I was a part of. I didn't directly contribute to his issue, but I didn't help it, either. My lack of knowledge of any of Catalan phrases with which I could ask for help, showed I didn't recognize his culture and cause.

I came into his home country, which he has a right to feel safe and comfortable in. What if he had terrible memories or an imprisoned family member from the protests that followed the failed referendum? That man had a right to his feelings, despite how big of an inconvenience they were for me. In the moment, I fielded his behavior, was polite in return, and didn't continue the trend of negativity.

If I expect others to respect my feelings, I have to recognize their right to express theirs as well. A lot of people forget this, though, and typically forget to give other people the courtesy they expect from them. It's easier to do things that you want to and avoid what you don't. That is, until you're on the other side of begging someone for basic human decency that they don't feel like you deserve.

This attitude is part of the ripple that fuels why so many people are still fighting for their rights. Whether it's racial equality, gender equality, LGBTQ+ rights, or other similar movements, in all of these cases, people just want basic decency. Once we accept that everyone has the right to their feelings, we can help further so many of these movements, because the ripple of this lesson when practiced, and the decency that comes with it, can influence a wave of people around you.

One way we can do this is by understanding the feelings of the people around us through our interpersonal relationships. As we'll come to learn, sometimes, there are just some relationships we cannot keep because they do not serve us. But there are ways we can accept this practice into those relationships, even if we're removing ourselves from them.

A really good example of this practice in our day and age can be found in modern-day dating. For those of you captured in its grasp, does the term "you don't owe them anything" ring a bell? It's become somewhat of a dating proverb, but it's a really unhealthy perspective to have about the people you bring into your life.

Recently, I was having a conversation with a group of friends in which one of them was venting about a guy she'd recently gotten involved with. Another friend advised her that she "didn't owe him anything" and encouraged her to avoid confronting the problem. They never had a "defining conversation" of what they were and the relationship was brief, so they both agreed she should just disengage without explanation from something she was complicit in creating. This situation is a common thing many people in my generation do called "ghosting" (And yes, I have been guilty of it.).

That friend and I had carpooled to the brewery we were at. Shortly after this conversation ended, we were walking back to her car. I still wasn't happy about the advice our other friends had given her, so I offered a more political way of handling it: I convinced her it would be easier to have a quick and honest conversation with the guy. Even if he wasn't happy to lose her, at least he had some type of closure that would allow him to move onto pursuing someone else.

She ended up following my advice, and it worked out well for her because he got the hint. Rather than wasting energy on trying to continue things with her, he left her alone within a few weeks and had less ill will toward her after everything was said and done (though he may have removed her as a friend on Snapchat).

Regardless, you DO owe people something, and that's because you owe it to yourself.

You owe yourself the right to have feelings, whether it's convenient or not. You owe yourself the right to express them. You owe yourself the closure that you need to heal and move on from life experiences, though my only stipulation is to be kind and lawful in your reactions. If you can recognize your right to these things, you can recognize why other people deserve to have them as well.

But, just like your feelings aren't always convenient, other people's feelings aren't always going to be convenient for you. That doesn't mean you should immediately invalidate them. Recognize them, and advocate for them, because you'd want the same done for you.

VI.

YOU CAN'T CONTROL EVERYTHING

The flight attendant smiled as we greeted her with a "good morning" on the way to our seats, a very small, but always appreciated, common courtesy to help ease any anxiety one may feel when getting on a plane. My friend and I were on our way home from a bachelorette party. We were exhausted but extremely excited to go home to our own beds, and of course, our loving four-legged companions. We dismissed the majority of the safety presentation the flight attendants are required to do prior to every takeoff, and we worked on some assignments as our plane rose above the thirty thousand-foot altitude it needed to reach to cruise.

Except, something felt off. As a frequent flier, I know to look at the faces of the flight attendants to gauge how I should be feeling. Since they do this for a living, they have a more telling reaction on if something, like turbulence, is normal or abnormal. I looked at the friendly face of the one that we greeted while we boarded the plane, and her facial expression seemed a little off to me.

I looked out of the window, and though I recognized I wasn't an expert, the objects in my view didn't seem as small as they usually would. Suddenly, I started hearing subtle reminders of the plane's safety features spoken through the intercom.

The trees in the window seemed to get larger, and the messages through the intercom were getting slightly more imperative every time the pilot came on. Finally, I heard a message that confirmed my suspicions.

"Folks, we have been trying to maintain the calm in the cabin, but we are unfortunately experiencing an electrical issue that has kept us from maintaining cruising altitude. We are being forced by our systems to make an emergency landing in an unpopulated forest. Please direct your attention to your flight attendants as they let you know what you must do to minimize your chances for a serious injury," he said.

I looked at my friend, and as the cabin masks dropped, we picked up the safety pamphlet and read it as we looked to the flight attendants for guidance.

The trees got bigger.

We braced ourselves for impact.

It hit.

The plane shook our bodies, while the sound of it all shook me to my core.

I hit my head, and it was over. We made it.

And then I woke up.

"NyQuil really messes with my head," I thought to myself as I noticed my heart rate was abnormally fast for someone who just woke up from a night's sleep.

Dreams have a poetic way of reminding us that we cannot control everything. This dream is one I recently had right before I flew back from a bachelorette party with the same friend from the dream. The actual flight, thankfully, did not have any issues or emergency landings. But if it had, I would have had a similar reaction to the one I had in the dream: keep calm, and do what you can to mitigate the impact.

Though we cannot control everything, we can learn how to better control our responses.

That being said, even your response is not something you'll always be able to *fully* control. Sometimes, your emotions become so overwhelming that you don't recognize who you become in the moment, and you may not know exactly why certain things affect you the way they do—an example of why we can't fully control our responses. In these instances, you must manage what you can, and learn from what you can't.

From there, we can begin to accept that we can't control everything, and that can be a good thing.

Even if you aren't someone who can openly acknowledge that you have struggles in your relationship with control, they may still be present in your life. Do you feel a sense of frustration when someone doesn't make a deadline at work that affects you? Or when you plan for something that doesn't happen? Or when a relationship or friendship turns sour?

Those frustrations come from not being at peace with the fact that all of those are things you can't control. They have the power to affect anyone's mood and disposition. But when you're more susceptible to external stimuli as someone who struggles with their mental health, little things can feel like the end of the world. It can trigger anger, sadness, and all sorts of negative reactions that cause you to lash out. But when you accept that you cannot control everything, you have a chance to remind yourself of that when you are subjected to something someone else is doing.

Breathe, absolve yourself from the situation mentally, and remember that it's not about you. Then focus on doing what you can to get through it.

Think about all the things that happen on a daily basis that we have no connection to. For me (to date this piece), I'm consumed by news of the Australian wildfires, the crisis with Iran, the potential of impeachment for our reigning president, and the budding coronavirus. Though I can react by voting in democratic elections, donating to charities that are helping fight the issue, avoiding any unnecessary travel, or overdosing on vitamin C (which is water-soluble, so no actual overdose is possible), I can't actually control these things on a personal level. But I forget that, so my mind will occasionally send me dreams about planes crashing to show me that I can't always control everything, but that doesn't mean I won't be okay.

Like we've mentioned, managing anything is a process. To accept what you can't control, you must acknowledge what you can. In moments like the ones in the above paragraph, you can only do some of those small acts, and then focus your energy on things that you have more power over. Sometimes, that means meditation, exercise, and mental preoccupation with something else to relieve the anxiety of coming to terms with an inability to control everything.

That doesn't mean that you can't find the silver lining in things you can't control. One such unfortunate case was the passing of my grandmother, when things that were out of my control allowed me to see her conscious one last time.

I wasn't supposed to see her before the surgery. It was a Wednesday, and I had scheduled a school engagement by the time my mom told me about it. But I didn't think it would be a problem, and I made sure to set aside time to come visit immediately after to see how she was doing. After all, it was just a simple procedure, nothing unplanned or life-threatening based on the doctor's professional advice.

On my way to the hospital, I called my mom to see how my grandma was doing, and she mentioned that the surgery had been delayed for three hours and she was a little anxious and tired, but it was something that was out of her control.

"I love you, and I'll see you two soon," I said.

When I got there, everything felt a little off. But I quickly felt more at ease when I reached my family. After hugging my grandma, I couldn't help but admire how much effort she put into getting ready for the surgery. She'd done her hair and makeup, ready to look great when she woke up, and had better blood flow to her legs.

After a half hour, the nurses came to bring her back to the operating room, and that's when my grandma started to cry. I realized then that she'd just been controlling her outward appearance, and I felt an ominous feeling as they rolled her wheelchair into the operating room.

The next twenty-four hours were a rollercoaster, so much so that it's still hard for me to have a good recollection of what timeline the following events took place in. At one point, we were told there were blood clots and that we'd have to amputate her legs to save her life. Then, shortly after, we were being told she'd never wake up. Her body transitioned to a deep yellow and purple color before we finally pulled the plug. It was awful, and we still believe it had to do with her care. We felt like we did everything right. We had great previous experiences with the hospital, and a physician friend had approved of the surgeon in charge of the surgery.

The worst part was that the surgery was elective, something she chose to do to improve blood flow to her feet and make walking less painful. We couldn't control her decision to have it, so we tried to control the environment she had it in through research and planning. Some things, we can't control, however, in moments like that one, it was especially hard to accept. We also couldn't control the late start to her surgery, but that uncontrollable twist was a silver lining that allowed me to see her one last time.

I try to control my surroundings, my body, my work, and yet accidents happen, sickness happens, and deadlines get missed. Even what seems to be controllable has an essence of free will.

People will make their decisions, they will affect you, and you won't always be able to control your response. Accept it, and find peace in knowing that your inability to control it is the reason why you're often unable to fully blame yourself for it, either.

VII.

SELF-CARE REQUIRES SACRIFICE

A street of duplexes passed through my peripheral view as I drove up on the grass lawn and parked my car behind a blue van. I took a deep breath, put my car in park, and enjoyed the silence before mustering up the courage to take my key out of the ignition and leave the safety of my car. I was about to enter what felt like a room full of people who hated me to be a part of a celebration that I would have regretted not attending.

Nothing is ever black and white, and celebratory moments are sometimes paired with the uncomfortable presence of shadows from the past. In this moment, someone I had a history with deliberately tried to exclude me from a celebratory event for a close mutual friend. Mustering up the courage to face this person, silence my anxious thoughts as I walked into a room of adversaries, and walk to the back of the room with my chin up was difficult. But the smile on my friend's face for making it there to support her made it worth it.

Had I missed it, I would have let my adversary hurt me, and I would have hurt myself with the regret of being an unsupportive friend. This event was a moment of self-care because I chose to sacrifice my immediate comfort and do something to support my long-term emotional health.

Self-care is something we do when we take care of our personal needs and promote our own emotional, mental, and physical health. However, society has romanticized and commercialized the idea of self-care by portraying it as nights in with face masks, bubble baths, and wine. Though a night with this trio of products can be the type of self-care you need in that moment, there is so much more to what self-care is. This widely adopted commercialized idea of it neglects to reflect how often it's paired with sacrifice. Taking care of yourself means you're taking on the role of being your own caretaker, and being a caretaker isn't easy.

If you ask any parent of a young child about their experience, they'll often state it's "hard, but rewarding." That's because caring for someone who isn't fully independent means bathing them, cleaning up their messes, and prioritizing their food and medicine over your own needs. But it's these sacrifices that help their children grow, and for any parent, that is the ultimate reward.

Being your own caretaker is a similar experience. It may mean making yourself go for a run when you have no motivation, losing sleep to meet a big deadline at work, paying the money you'd spend on those face masks, bubble baths, and wine; toward a student loan debt, or choosing to work on book revisions to avoid cramming the last few days before the deadline instead of video-chatting and drinking wine with your friends. In the end, it's the best thing for your long-term health and growth. But in the moment, it's not always the comfortable idea that we envision self-care to be.

I've had to go through many periods of sacrifice-induced self-care to support many different life goals. The main thing it's taught me is that you have to approach self-care strategically, and the self-care actions you partake in are most beneficial when they revolve around your goals.

As a strategic communications consultant, I tell my clients that an "effective" communications strategy will look unique for every single client. They can apply the same basic principles to it, but the one that works for them is uniquely based on their goals.

In applying this lesson to our lives, we must accept that in addition to knowing we can't control everything, we have to guide the actions we can control by the life goals of what we really want. Thus, when it comes to figuring out how to tackle your self-care regimen, you have to ask yourself that exact question: What do you want?

Trying to answer this question for myself has been difficult, as I've been at a constant crossroads between my desire to be influential in my professional goals and maintaining meaningful relationships with friends, families, and romantic partners.

Over the years, I've learned to apply my professional knowledge in my personal life. Just like I segment my clients' communication targets into two to four segments of demographics, I do the same with my life goals. Though they, like mental health management techniques, will change over time, they can still steer decisions during the present moment in your life.

Right now, I define my goals as the following:

1. Finish my graduate degree
2. Be a high-performer at work
3. Maintain healthy friendships
4. Stay physically healthy

So, if I have to make a sacrifice, I question how the options at hand would affect any of these goals.

Touching upon my job again, it's something I covet because it allows me opportunities to travel, and meet and network with many successful people who expose me to new challenges and experiences. Achieving it was my most important life goal a year ago, and it came with sacrifices of friendships, sleep, and health.

Maintaining my goal of being a high performer in my job translates to long days, impromptu travel requirements, 5 a.m. flights, doing homework on planes, and missing dinners and events, which can strain my relationships at times. I wouldn't trade it, but I have to remind myself of how difficult it can be to work on chapters in this book or get my weekly graduate school assignments turned in when my brain is fried from a fifty-hour week.

Additionally, I've learned that the sacrifices you make can have a ripple effect. You have to understand there is more to what you're giving up than what may initially present itself on the surface level. You have a chance to choose what matters to you by setting your goals. Therefore, you can choose what, and how much, you may lose in the face of self-care-induced sacrifice.

In your situation, it may mean having to miss a party or a special occasion because of a looming deadline. Or, on the contrary, it could mean passing up a promotion or setting work-life balance boundaries that make you get passed over for one to be able to focus on your family. It's understanding what's important to you that allows you to choose.

For me, those long weeks and workloads have meant I've made bad impressions on people whom I acted like a zombie around because of my fatigue. It's also meant that I've started combining my quality time with friends with running errands by doing them together, or I've chosen to take a lower grade instead of being a perfectionist on all my assignments to be a good friend while also getting the medically recommended amount of sleep.

But understanding your priorities, coupled with also understanding how you best manage your symptoms, allows you to mitigate how much you have to sacrifice. Having a full workload may mean you adapt (like I do) by practicing excellent time management skills and living and breathing by a planner. If an important event has popped up that is imperative to my goal of maintaining healthy friendships, I can schedule homework for an extra thirty minutes a night leading up to the event to get some extra work done. The thirty minutes I lose in sleep isn't marginally significant enough to affect my goal of staying physically healthy, but it can free up two hours for me to attend the event if I know four days in advance.

In the scenario that opened this chapter, the uncomfortable presence of a few adversaries at the event was something I mitigated by taking deep breaths in the car and drinking wine to calm my nerves as soon as I entered the building. I may have sacrificed some comfort throughout the night, but I didn't sacrifice any of the goals that matter to me most.

Your goals may be very different from mine, and your coping strategies may be as well. But the thought process around determining your priorities, and the core lesson of accepting that your self-care may require sacrifice, applies to us all. Many morals, goals, and responsibilities make up who you are as an individual. You have the power to choose which ones you can prioritize and give your attention to.

Not having healthy expectations for self-care can lead to you negating growth by fixating on the disappointment that comes from the sacrifices you often have to make. Concurrently, not recognizing what's truly important to you can cause you to make the wrong sacrifices for your long-term benefit. Not everyone wants to be a CEO. For some people, physical health may be the most important thing. We're all unique, and so are our goals and ambitions. The things that constitute self-care for us, and the sacrifices we're willing to make, are just as unique as our minds.

Learn to identify your needs and your desires as they change, and work to both achieve them and mitigate the sacrifices you'll have to make. Self-care is a beautiful thing, but it's not always pretty, and accepting that can really help you manage your expectations with it.

VIII.

KINDNESS IS THE ANSWER, BUT THAT DOESN'T ALWAYS MEAN BEING NICE

I had everything timed out perfectly for the evening. I left work at 4 p.m., finished yoga by 5:30 p.m., and was in route with my roommate to attend my friend's birthday dinner that started at 6:30 p.m. I made sure to hit all my bases, and I was planning on having a great night (even when I accept that I can't control everything, I still have high hopes).

That was, until I turned into the mall where the restaurant was located. I had my eyes on the road and all of a sudden, I heard a loud bump that sounded like something collided into my car. I looked around in shock, feeling as if I couldn't be responsible for hitting anything. I saw the car behind me signal for me to turn into a parking lot to assess the damage.

When we parked, the couple immediately jumped out of the car and started yelling at me. "Oh honey, you hit us. I'm going to get your information. If there's any damage, you're going to have to pay for this," the woman sneered.

Well, after having a few seconds to process what just happened, I determined they had actually hit me while swerving between traffic lanes. But they were attempting to take advantage of two young-looking females by making me believe the blame was on me. The woman even had the nerve to tell me she "got it on video" and pointed to her camera.

Having grown up with a mother who always said this even when it wasn't true, I called her on her bluff: "If you have it on video, let me see the video. But also, why were you filming a video on your cell phone of your partner driving? And considering you hit me from the back, I was centered in my lane, and only one side of your car hit mine, that means you must have swerved into the lane."

The woman refused to show me her phone, and immediately they seemed nervous. They realized the scare tactic and the patronizing "honey" wasn't enough to get me to fearfully submit to them in that confrontation.

But after assessing the very minimal scratches they put on my car, I decided to let them go. I knew that situation could have gone very differently had I succumbed to their threats, so I patted myself on the back for not being nice. But I also knew the damage wasn't anything more than a few scratches, and I saw that behind the heated words was a scared couple who seemed to have something else on their minds. Knowing I let them go reminded me of the importance of choosing my battles and the importance of kindness in responding to someone who's stressed and emotional.

One thing I've learned in life is that kindness is always the answer, but that doesn't always mean being nice.

Now, you may be wondering what the difference between the two is. Being nice revolves around *pleasing people*, whereas kindness revolves around *doing things with care*. You can care for someone and have their best interests at heart, yet still not please them with your actions.

Think back to the last chapter on self-care, in which we mentioned that being a caretaker isn't always easy. It has a lot to do with this concept. Sometimes a disconnect is found between doing things with care in what we assume to be in someone's best interest, and doing what makes them happy. This philosophy is extremely important for parents raising their children.

Being in my twenties, I love my parents and genuinely enjoy spending time with them (with a few faux pas in conversation such as my romantic life or my mental illness). That's because I've landed on my feet, and I support and take care of myself. That burden of being a caretaker has been alleviated from them, and our relationship doesn't involve the strains it used to. But the constant pressure of fighting with them, feeling like they were always making things difficult for me, and all those all too common teenage perceptions were the way I'd describe my relationship with them up until a few years ago.

I may not agree with them on every decision they've made, and objectively, some decisions they made were not the right ones for me. They're only human, after all. But every single one prioritized my health and my education, even if they made me unhappy at the time.

One parenting decision my mom made when I was twelve is something I still use as a great example of this concept. I was going through a phase in which I wanted snake bite piercings, and I was crying and arguing with her over it.

My mom also knew that the desktop computer I wrote all my stories and did all my homework on was old and slow. Writing has always been my passion, and I was starting to lose the tool that allowed me to do it.

So, she proposed that she would get me a laptop for my upcoming birthday if I promised I'd NEVER get snake bites. Was I happy about agreeing to "NEVER" do something I wanted? No. But I accepted the terms and I got my laptop. A year later, I was still using that laptop (it lasted four years), but I was eternally grateful I never pierced my face because I fell out of that fashion phase and would have been appalled to have those piercings.

I was especially complimentary of her at her method of using the laptop as collateral. Realistically, my brother was an adult and could have helped me get the piercings by giving permission as "my legal guardian" at a tattoo and piercing shop. I also had the opportunity to have some girl pierce them with a needle in the middle school bathroom (yes, she was a real person). But giving me something that was related to something I love prevented me from cashing my piggy bank of coins at my local Publix and making it happen. That's because the tools she provided me afforded me something I didn't want to risk. My mom was kind in her response of supporting a healthy habit, but didn't care if I thought she was nice by shutting down my fashion choices.

Sometimes, it's a concept that can't be applied as light-heartedly. I think of a friend I had in my adolescence who opened up to me about a past relationship that ended very poorly. She'd been in a relationship with someone who dealt with a lot of unresolved mental health issues that manifested into behaviors that made him extremely emotionally abusive toward her. He would obsessively call her when she was out with friends if she didn't text him back within a few minutes of receiving his message, he would make rude and embarrassing comments about her appearance in front of her friends, and he would guilt her with threats of self-harm anytime she talked about wanting to leave the relationship. Naturally, she didn't want him to hurt himself, so she stayed in the relationship, which she admitted enabled him to treat her worse as time went on.

One day, she'd finally had enough. He had gotten into an argument with her mom and called her a few choice words. She told me her tolerance for his mistreatment did not extend to anyone else, and that seeing him be verbally aggressive with her mom was her breaking point. When they got back to his home, she went inside with him and told him she was done. As she was grabbing her things to leave, he grabbed a fork, and the next thing she heard was a scream. It caught her attention, and she realized that he had stabbed himself in the leg with it and punctured his skin.

She made eye contact with him, and he started crying.

"It's all your fault," he screamed.

She was shocked, but not stunned. She quickly exited the home and pulled out her phone as soon as she got outside.

Out of the love and care she had for him, she did him one final service. She called 911 to report his act of puncturing his skin and prompted police to Baker Act him for his safety and to ensure he was monitored and got the help he needed. Once the police got there and handled the situation, she left, doing herself the ultimate service. For anyone unfamiliar with Baker Acting, it is a Florida statute that allows you to have someone involuntarily institutionalized if they meet predetermined criteria so they can have emergency care given to them regarding their mental health.[45]

He wasn't happy with her, but after seeing him physically act on his threats, she knew he needed help. Her actions were done with care for him and done with care for herself by leaving and not allowing him to push his negativity onto her. But I'm sure if you ever ask him his side of the story, he doesn't refer to her Baker Acting him as a "nice" act.

We haven't kept in touch, but her story reminded me of the importance of this lesson and serves as a reminder whenever I feel like I'm falling into a people-pleasing mode at my own expense. This problem tends to be especially true for me as a young professional at work who wants to do well and advance in my career. As I mentioned, I sacrifice a lot at times to be a high performer. I have a hard time saying no, and I find myself editing and creating documents late at night, doing favors for coworkers on weekends, sending emails at 4 a.m., and having my coworkers joke at eight in the morning that my Skype said I've only been offline for a few hours.

But as many of us may identify with, I've missed out on birthday dinners, family time, and a lot of other important events, which has caused me to learn to, at least, set some parameters to my workaholism. Sometimes the kindness and care can mean delegating a task, or being upfront about how long the turnaround time can be, even if the one tasking me isn't pleased about it.

---

45   "The 2019 Florida Statutes: Chapter 394: Mental Health," Statutes & Constitution: View Statutes: Online Sunshine, The Florida Legislature, accessed on May 14, 2020.

We all want to make the people in our lives happy. But sometimes, someone's happiness isn't best for them, or for us. Focusing on pleasing people can cause us to enable their bad behaviors or force us to personally sacrifice things that hurt us in the end. But that also doesn't mean that we should dismiss people, because we do owe them basic decency. So, if you care for someone, show it in your actions. As long as you are kind, things tend to work out in the end.

IX.

THIS TOO SHALL PASS

Eleven o'clock had struck, and a notification popped up on my computer: it was time for a meeting to discuss what a website for my book would look like. My mom's good friend had scheduled a call with me, herself, and her husband who has a plethora of professional advice and experience on the topic.

"Hello!" I started with enthusiasm. "Thank you for your time today."

"Of course! We're driving up to Washington, DC, so thank you for being flexible," she responded.

"Ooh, are you going to see anything fun while you're up there? I love DC!" I responded.

"We go a lot, so not too much sightseeing. I will, however, walk by the White House and flick off our lovely president."

"Woah! You better watch out for those snipers on the edges of each corner," I warned her.

"You think I'm afraid of snipers?" she questioned.

"Aren't we all?" I asked.

"No. Back in the war, I once had to cross a bridge that we were told we'd get shot at by snipers if we entered. But I had no other way to get where I needed, so my friend and I ran across the bridge as quickly as we could, and they started shooting. But every single shot missed. So, as I ran, I put up my middle finger in the direction where the shots were coming from and screamed, 'Fuck you!'"

I paused for a second. Then we got down to talking business.

Reflecting on this story, I think about how in any difficult life situation we're faced with, it can feel like the end of the world. What her perspective taught me was that she didn't die, and, for any situation I've been in, neither have I.

Back in high school, I remember being part of a conversation with some upperclassmen regarding the tattoos everyone was planning on getting when they turned eighteen. Truthfully, I don't remember the majority of the answers, but there is one in particular I do remember.

One of the girls started talking about a tattoo of text she wanted on her lower rib cage, stating "This Too Shall Pass." Then, she went on to say that in her short life, she'd experienced quite a few losses and heartbreaks. What she learned early on was that everything, good and bad, passed eventually, and so when some of the harder losses and moments occurred, the only thing that got her through the pain was knowing "this too shall pass."

It stuck with me.

Part of accepting you have a problem is also accepting there is a way to move past it.

Accepting you're in pain, you're lacking, or you're sad is only constructive if you simultaneously accept that "this too shall pass."

Think about it. What's the point of accepting you have a negative quality or a defining trauma if there isn't a way to navigate through it or improve it? It would be a pretty depressing and ineffective coping method, especially since lying to yourself about your flaws can at least encourage you to do some kind things, albeit for the wrong reasons.

This concept manifests itself in many ways, but to accept it, it's best to explore it in my three favorite categories: the good, the bad, and the ugly.

THE GOOD: FLEETING HAPPY MOMENTS

Some of our happiest moments are the simplest ones. I've had a lot of great memories, but one odd one that stands out as a moment of pure bliss was at a Zedd concert. I lived on my college campus, and I found out Zedd was coming to the University of South Florida (USF) Sun Dome (now known as the Yuengling Center). Since it was on campus, a few of my friends and I were able to pregame and get a sustainable buzz going.

We walked over to the arena and made our way to the pit, where we got a spot very close to the stage. The concert was a blur of singing along to my favorite hits, and for the final song, my friend picked me up unexpectedly and somehow got me on his shoulders. The view from there was incredible, and it was during my favorite song of Zedd's at the time. All of a sudden, he changed the lights and fired some type of decorations from a cannon.

I just remember being lost in the music, amazed by the lights, and completely in awe of the beauty of the moment. It was something I knew would end and I'd only have my memory of, so I savored the moment of that little unexpected gem.

Now, I've had plenty of other moments I could list as moments that felt perfect. But the reason why this one was so touching was because of how unexpected it was. If I spend thousands of dollars on a trip to Europe, there is a certain degree of expectation that comes with it. But when the cost of the night was a thirty-dollar ticket and a handle of vodka, I didn't expect much of a return. Regardless, when I felt it, I recognized how fleeting it was, and how no picture or video would have done it justice. Thus, I avoided any distractions and indulged in it until it passed.

There is a comfort in knowing all good things come to an end. If you recognize the sweetness of these moments touching your heart cannot last forever, you're more likely to give them your full attention and savor them in the fullest way. Knowing their finite nature also helps mitigate the grief you may feel once it's over, since it's something you knew to expect.

THE BAD: TRAGEDIES IN LIFE

One of my best friends is someone who survived a battle with cancer before I met her. It always intrigued me how positive she was and how nonchalant her tone was when discussing what she went through. One day, I finally asked her about her experience for this book, and she shared screenshots of a Facebook post she'd made after she went into remission, prior to participating in a Relay for Life event.

In it, she described how hard it was to go through. She woke up crying for weeks after her diagnosis. The chemotherapy made her immune system so weak that she was constantly fighting infections at the site of her biopsies. She was unable to get on a plane to fly home for Christmas and went through moments of uncontrollably puking on herself as a side effect of the treatments.

She always notes that she was lucky in her diagnosis. For her diagnosis, there was a very high chance of going into long-term remission (80 percent), and she had just moved to a city that had one of the best cancer centers in the country within a thirty-minute drive. It helped her to know her odds were good, but it didn't alleviate the anxiety of potentially being in the 20 percent who weren't able to go into long-term remission.

Additionally, losing her hair was one of the hardest things for her. It felt like she lost a bit of her womanhood on top of all the pain.

But hair grows back, and that's symbolic for the difficult things that pass in our life.

In getting through the tragedies, some moments are uncomfortable, painful, and devastating. Being positive and knowing the pain will pass is not only good for your mental health in those scenarios, but also necessary for your survival.

THE UGLY: DEALING WITH YOURSELF.
Sometimes, it's our own self-reflection that leads us to find we are at fault for some negative things in our lives. Whether that is due to bad decisions, bad habits, or bad actions, the truth of knowing that the only one who can accept blame for an outcome is you, is ugly.

I've done things I'm not proud of. I've overreacted to situations and responded childishly. I sometimes judge people and situations too soon and say hurtful things. Most of the time, it's to a trusted confidant, but the negativity still escapes my lips. I'll admit as many times as you want me to that I'm not perfect. But what makes it easier to accept is that I also know I'm always growing.

The person I am today is calmer, wiser, and kinder than the one I was at this time last year, and increasingly so the farther back we go. There is a comfort in knowing that when

I recognize a negative quality of mine, I can make a plan to improve it and know it too shall pass.

Just like everything else.

Which is what pushes me to carry on, and apparently what can give you the courage to run through a field while actively avoiding shots from snipers.

X.

FRIENDS MAY SAY THEY WANT THE WORLD FOR YOU, BUT ONLY IF IT'S ONE THEY CAN ENVISION

When you're lonely, it feels like your vision is clouded.

Imagine you're driving through a fog, and then you see a crossroads.

One path is familiar to you. It's flat, but the fog is so thick that, despite your knowledge of it, you're afraid to take it. This path represents a path of continued loneliness. The other path is visible, with little to no mist, but you see sharp turns, potholes, and varying elevation. This path represents a path with a companion, though one that may not be right for you. Desperate for unclouded vision, you take the path you can see, despite the red flags.

Sometimes, we meet people in our lives who offer us something we want, and in spite of red flags, we accept it. Eventually, the negatives take a toll on us, and we want to steer onto a different path. A lot of the people involved don't take it lightly, assuming you are indebted to them for their part in getting you out of your fog.

I've had some former friends who fit the role of this path. When I was vulnerable, and clouded, and in desperate need of a friend, they offered me the opportunity to clear the fog and let out the thoughts that clouded my vision. However, this relief came at the cost of the hazards they put me through. Once you deviate from this path, you're punished with a fall that the flat road would have never given you.

These were the same friends who would say they would do anything for me and that they wanted to give me the world. I believed them and allowed them to become integral parts of my journey. I offered them support, friendship, and the benefits of my success. But once I started deviating from them and the image they created of me in their head, I realized how conditional their friendship and support were.

About two years ago, I met a girl at a bar. She was friends with all of my mutual friends, and she immediately wanted to start spending a lot of time together. I was initially a little hesitant, but she persisted, and finally, she was rewarded. A few months later, I was in a dark and lonely place, and I felt the fog begin to thicken. It was at this vulnerable time that she offered me the other path.

I noticed early on that she wasn't a great listener, and she was pretty self-righteous. It seemed as if anything that didn't completely cater to her needs was wrong. Rather than trying to understand my needs, she tried to force her perspectives onto me. It started to become exhausting, but I fell into a pattern of accepting the drama in exchange for her friendship.

One evening, we met up at a concert with a big group of friends. She had Ubered there, and I had driven. After the show ended, though I knew I was coherent to drive, I couldn't help but be a little anxious about leaving the venue (which was surrounded by cops) because of the two beers I had during the show. While I was mentally calming myself down, she started asking me to fit her and her friends into my already full car. When I told her no and explained that it was illegal, my car windows weren't tinted, and I had been drinking, she started to bully me and call me a selfish friend for making her and her other friends split an Uber.

I stood firm in my decision, expressing how selfish it was of her to put me in an at-risk position of a ticket, points on my license, or a DUI. She kept berating me in front of everyone, and it was a wake-up call for me as to how much her own self-interest overshadowed my well-being.

She had a certain vision of who I was to her and what role I played in her world. In her world, she expected me to put myself in uncomfortable positions to prove my loyalty and friendship to her. This view contradicted with my view of how friendships should be and how "testing" your friend's devotion and loyalty makes for an unhealthy relationship.

This interaction made me realize those expectations she had were beginning to impose on my life. I wasn't willing to put myself at risk for her because that wasn't the expectation I had of my own friends. I couldn't force myself to meet her expectations, and ultimately, that meant that the "world" she'd promised me was one she'd never help me reach.

As a result, my response was to respectfully distance myself and to try to maintain a relationship with her that didn't create too many opportunities for these disagreements to arise.

She, in turn, started to make passive-aggressive comments, telling me that all my other friends were phases, and purposely trying to ruin my day and avoid doing things with me. Then, when her actions didn't warrant her the attention she felt like she deserved, she started trying to sabotage my other friendships, eventually getting to other people in my life.

Throughout this period, I kept trying to smooth things over. I wanted to be nice because I felt a loyalty to her for being there for me through a really rough time. That was until she started throwing the fact that she was there for me in my face, and telling me I used her and replaced her.

It made the less frequent interactions more difficult to stomach, and I was beginning to realize a clean cut was going to be the response I had to take. It was frustrating feeling like I couldn't do anything right, and it was awful to feel like I was being punished for going down a path that was better for me and for my mental health.

But that's what made me realize she wasn't a true friend.

True friendship isn't conditional. You may have needs one person can't meet, so you can go and find the fulfillment to those needs in someone else. You can still love another friend whose world doesn't align with yours and accept a more distant type of friendship. True friends are happy to see you grow, despite any discontent they may feel when they feel like they're losing you. Especially if these friends wanted the world for you.

Realizing this definition of true friendship has been one of the most valuable lessons in creating an effective network of support. Feeling the love and care of these friends, without strings attached or animosity, is the kind of love that can make you want to heal and be a better person for them. In other words, it can be the thing that makes you want to get better, which is the most important part of the healing journey.

A lot of friends in your life aren't going to be selflessly happy for your success, especially when they are feeling as if they're lacking in their own. When there's someone who promises you the world, just be careful to see what they envision as the world they want to give. If you find yourself in draining situations, accept it, set boundaries, and sever it if all else fails.

When I deviated from her path, she punished me for it. I wasted time and energy trying to figure out what I did wrong and being upset by her childish behavior. But finally, I accepted I couldn't live in the world she envisioned, and I moved on.

It's easier to heal from clouded vision than a fall off a jagged cliff.

XI.

PEOPLE WILL LEAVE YOUR LIFE, AND FIGHTING IT WILL DO MORE HARM THAN GOOD

A common theme I explore and touch on a lot in this book is losing people I care about. It's an unfortunate universal experience everyone on this planet will suffer through, and likely more than once.

For those of us who suffer from mental disorders, we sometimes become our own worst enemies and allow our symptoms and tunnel vision to manifest into behaviors that push the people in our lives away. For myself, it could mean a heightened sense of irritability that causes me to lash out on loved ones; or a spiral into a depression that forces me to push my friends away; or my control issues arising and scaring new people in my life.

Knowing we're at fault for these dissolutions can sometimes lead us to have an unhealthy fixation with the breakdown of these relationships. But what I've come to find is that many times, you can't pin the blame on yourself, even though those of us who suffer from the heightened self-criticism that mental illness brings are extremely good at it.

We begin to overcompensate and sometimes fight the processing of a loss, and we hold onto the relationship with rose-colored goggles. Sometimes, we're so invested in the idea of saving what we've romanticized so much that we're unable to recognize what the role of the relationship was, and if that role still has a purpose in our lives.

People will leave your life.

Now this doesn't mean your long-term relationships with friends, associates, family members, and romantic partners will stand without effort. There will always be difficult times and disagreements, and it takes two to compromise, grow, and move past those times.

This lesson of accepting that people will leave your life is referring to those relationships that begin to feel problematic and drain you more often than they benefit you.

"It all started so well," you may think. "We have to be able to get back there. There's something I can do. How did we even get here?"

Sometimes people fill a certain role in our lives. That role may spring up out of convenience to both parties. It may be the by-product of favorable situations, or just the harmony of two individuals' life stages aligning. As an example, college students become very close when they spend all their time studying for the same class together. These close friendships help them academically survive, and emotionally deal with the stress they go through. But once the semester is over, they may find it too difficult to maintain relationships with old classmates, and move onto a new group. In this instance, they completed the role they were supposed to fulfill in each other's lives.

Everything is dynamic. Situations change, and so do people. What once felt great and seemed like it would last forever may suddenly feel like it never fit in the first place. Nothing goes the way that it used to, and you end up feeling frustrated and like you're unable to do anything right with that person anymore. This situation tends to happen because we still want that person to fit a role they simply cannot fulfill on their end, or maybe that role just doesn't seem to exist in your life anymore.

If you're still in the developmental stages of your life, you may grow apart more often than those who are settled do. For example, you may have a "work spouse" who is your best friend and confidant forty-plus hours of the week. Let's say you move to a different company, and your role involves a lot more work, and less drama, than the last role did. You get lunch with your former work spouse and suddenly see there isn't really anything you two have in common anymore.

Your relationship was based off the convenience of schedules and the common need to vent about your coworkers. That situation no longer applies, and you realize you've outgrown the need for that role. You can still love the person, but maintaining a friendship with them may mean infrequently seeing them or having to find another thing in common with each other.

It's like trying to fit a square block into a circular hole. You can shove it with all your might, you can saw at the sides of the hole, or you can try to physically alter the square block to make it work.

Or, you could put the square block into a square-shaped hole, and find yourself a sphere to put in the circular one.

Fighting the fact that sometimes people outgrow each other will do more harm than good.

We must recognize when things aren't a fit for us anymore, even if they used to be.

The hardest part is that in the case of people, there's not always a specific situation or event you can fault for the breakdown of a relationship. At times, it could very well even be amicable. But for many of us, that lack of fault is something we struggle with, and it leaves us with feelings that are unresolved.

Many of us can't run marathons (I will happily stick to my mindset of considering two miles a long-distance run). But, oh boy, our minds sure can. To get them to stop running, we have to have a finish line for them. This finish line is what we associate with our concept of "closure." When there is no fault or blame at the end of a relationship, we're left with too many "what ifs." It's as if the marathon in our mind has been placed in an unmarked forest. Without any indication of where that finish line is, we could loop around in search of it forever.

If we never cross that finish line and leave that forest, we become stuck in it, just like those who cannot let go of past relationships who become stuck in the past with them. That forest becomes a place of comfort as we run around it every day and learn all of its ins and outs. Even when we begin to see the path toward a finish line align, we become scared of what we see on the other side: an unfamiliar place. As such, we fight the new terrain and hold onto our forest, even though we begin to literally run in circles.

Staying in the past may feel comfortable, and holding onto people you've outgrown may feel more comfortable than letting the relationship go. But staying in the past halts your timeline, and after enough stagnation, it taints the progression of your future.

Let's say all of the running you're doing has caused you to develop really severe shin splints. To keep going, you've found ways to mask the pain. You started stretching, running your circles on softer terrains, and running in intervals. You've gotten comfortable in your habits. But across the finish line is a physical therapist, and they have a program that can heal your chronic shin splints. Yet your comfort keeps you stuck in the past behind the finish line, and ultimately keeps you from a healthier future with a happier daily experience.

This concept applied with people plays out in a similar way. We sometimes stay in relationships that aren't right for us anymore, and that can involve having to go out of our way to remain relevant. Let's say that when we realize we don't have much in common with our former work spouse, and, rather than trying to see what new role they can fulfill, we focus our energy on the "venting" that used to keep us together.

We spend energy listening to them talk about our former coworkers and preoccupy our minds with what they're doing. To contribute, we start trying to find more gossip and drama in our new companies to share. We could spend this time and thought on topics related to our passions and desires, but instead, we're dedicating it to distracting negative thoughts.

To accept our issues in a way that allows us to move forward through a process of healing and managing our symptoms progressively, we must be willing to make necessary changes. These changes could very well mean leaving behind a relationship that's become unhealthy, as I discussed in the past chapter about friendships.

Regardless of what it is, it's hard to leave behind what we feel defines us, but accepting that everything, and everyone, changes is a first step. By recognizing some changes no longer have a place in your life, that's not a bad reflection on you; it can allow you to let it go.

The greatest accomplishments and relationships of your life are waiting for you. You just have to make sure you keep their place open. If you keep yourself in the past, you'll fill your life with things, and people, that aren't right for you. So if you see something isn't good for your health anymore, change it, and welcome the positive change it will bring you.

A CONNECTION
(ACCEPT TO REFLECT)

I come to you with a mission. And that is to illustrate how quickly someone can go from never experiencing mental illness to having it take over their life and to, as a result, attempting to take their life.

You can feel hopeless when you feel broken, when you feel deficient. When you look at a set of pills that act like vitamins for your mind but with torturous side effects, and then they tell you it's a life sentence. Sometimes these side effects are the by-product of being fed an unfitting medication, and yet not many doctors seem to have found an efficient way of figuring out what the right fit is without the painful trial and error.

Unlike a lot of things in our society, mental illness doesn't discriminate. You could be rich, famous, world-renowned, ideologically beautiful, successful, and a motivation to others, but be deeply and utterly depressed, or so anxious you're unable to function. And the loneliest part of it all, is that it isn't obvious to others.

Acceptance is the first step to recognizing you have a problem, and it's also the first step to allow healing mindsets and actions to come into your life. I have a friend from college who shared his journey of accepting a newly manifested set of symptoms associated with his mental illness. During this journey, he went through a great deal of reflections that serve as a connection into my own.

He's a friend who, during college, I hadn't really ever had too many conversations with, but we always had a lot of mutual respect for each other. When I reached out to my network asking for stories and experiences with mental illness, he was one of the first to respond and share his. I found we had both been suffering in silent solidarity throughout the time we knew each other. He was someone who, unbeknownst to me, attempted to take his life during that period, and I hadn't known anything about it until I began this research.

His journey began three years ago when he first began to suffer from symptoms of uncontrollable depression and anxiety. As someone who was academically inclined, philanthropic, creative, and in many ways accomplished, he never thought he'd fall into the debilitating symptoms of mental illness.

It began with weakness and clamminess, and over the course of the coming weeks, it progressed into debilitating episodes with seemingly no trigger. Finally, seeing a need for professional help, he got what he viewed as his life sentence: severe generalized anxiety, severe panic disorder, and mild depression. For anyone who has heard the term "bad things come in threes," this diagnosis definitely fit the bill. Which began his rollercoaster of a journey.

I went through periods of weeks to months where my anxiety was controllable, and subsequently went through periods where I could hardly cope. My depression would fluctuate similarly, in line with how severe my anxiety was being.

But life stops for no one, and throughout the discomfort, he carried on. He was paying attention to his diet, working to notice triggers, and taking his prescribed medications. However, he was also hiding his condition from employers and anyone he thought might limit him or treat him differently because of his condition. Unfortunately, masking the problem only made it worse.

When having severe anxiety for weeks on end, the exhaustion caused by simply existing would heighten the feelings of emptiness and depression.

With the use of coping skills and medications, he felt himself feeling some victories little by little as time went on. But the hopelessness lingered. Nothing seemed to do more than mask the problem, and the frustration of not being able to get a good grasp on a long-term solution for his mental health was turning into resentment. This heightened the feeling of the mental up and down that had become his new normal.

Finally, one year ago, he hit his breaking point.

I genuinely felt that my brain was failing me and my body was following.

Experiencing a week of unbearable anxiety, panic attacks, and general weakness that made it difficult to exist, he decided it was time to end the difficulty by attempting to take his life and hanging himself in his apartment closet from a metal wall shelving. But as he lost consciousness, the brain and the body that he felt were failing him showed a resilience to live, and saved him.

After losing consciousness I must have been thrashing around like crazy because I came to sometime later on my closet floor with the shelf broken off from the wall and on top of me. My psychiatrist arranged for me to get checked out for brain damage due to it but I was lucky and did not suffer lasting effects.

He survived and was grateful, and I am grateful, too. Because waking up to light when you expected darkness is an experience that evokes a lot of gratitude, and like our silent solidarity in suffering, we shared that same solidarity in being grateful.

Life and consciousness are forever fleeting, and the desire for the inevitable in dying can be stronger in those of us who feel a lack of stability in other aspects of our living lives. Death is something we will all go through, and when someone feels like their life is spiraling out of their control, they may desire for it to come sooner than they originally anticipated. For some, it's a fleeting thought, for others, it becomes an attempt at pushing up their own timeline.

Healing isn't easy, but it's a journey, and we're all doing it together, and sometimes, the gratification of peace of mind is delayed.

My friend will admit to you that, though in a better place with a wonderfully understanding support system and more knowledge of the behaviors that consistently attribute to his episodes, life is significantly harder than it was before depression and anxiety.

I can't remember what it feels like to be fully free from a day of anxiety or of depression entirely. And though I have to admit that I've had a hard time of viewing it as anything but a negative, the one noticeable "advantage" I've gained from the years of dealing with severe anxiety is an acute ability of self-awareness and awareness of others, what's taking place around me, and how others are perceiving others and I.

Although it's hard, he's a kinder and more thoughtful person for it. His actions are making the world a better place, one positive and thoughtful exchange with a stranger at a time. His motivation to heal and get better is pushing him to be a leader in trying new technologies that may eventually become a common solution for those who suffer from the same issues.

Something slightly less known that I have started recently is neurofeedback therapy. As the brain is the only organ in the body that can't repair itself without some kind of blueprint, neurofeedback is my best bet for long-term mental health improvement. You're basically hooked up to an EEG reading your brain waves, and it translates the data into fractal images and sounds that show your brain a blueprint of how it should be functioning. Over time the hope is that my brain will take that blueprint and slowly adjust itself to a more "normal" system. After a few sessions now, I'm feeling very optimistic that it will create results I've been looking for but never found yet.

He's healing, as we all are, and is a kinder person for it, with empathy and a sense of self-awareness that's contributed to his growth. But the darkness of mental illness can happen to anyone, and it's not just a thought in your head that you can change.

For every person reading this, know you're not alone, you're not selfish, you're not crazy, and you're not whatever you think you are for your thoughts. You're a human being who's in pain, and your natural instincts to stop the pain are kicking in. But you're unique, valuable, and irreplaceable, and you deserve to reach out for the help you need when you feel pain, even if it means calling the National Suicide Prevention Lifeline at 1-800-273-8255.

Don't let the world miss out on you, and don't let your soul miss out on loving every bit of who you are, and who you will inevitably become in your long and prosperous life.

REFLECT

I.
'REFLECT' INTRODUCTION

In the battle with mental illness, there is so much power in understanding how you and your illness intertwine. If you lack this understanding, you become a bystander to your own life. But the only way to gain this understanding is through thoughtful reflection.

I've watched my symptoms continuously change over time. Years ago, they could manifest into irregular heart palpitations induced by insomnia, panic attacks, or bedridden-ing mental and physical exhaustion from the act of being alive. Nowadays, it could be any of these, or newer manifestations like the inability to focus, uncontrollable crying spells, or gastrointestinal problems (like intestinal bleeding) that have, at times, put wrenches in my plans and made me afraid to leave my home.

Now that we've taken a section to discuss some of the technical knowledge behind mental illness and touched upon basic lessons that, once accepted, make managing it a little less difficult, we can explore the effects certain feelings and themes have on those with mental illness based on me and my journey with managing my bipolar disorder. A lot of the themes we'll explore in this next section are dedicated to feelings (i.e. love, happiness, anger, anxiety), and some are observations on overarching themes that have affected me in my journey (i.e. grief shaming, context, forgiveness, self-reflection, accountability).

But the most important part of this section of chapters is the exploration of finding the underlying lesson in each story of how I got to learning the root of **why** I was feeling and behaving certain ways, and **what** I could do about it.

Understanding what is more likely to trigger your symptoms to flare up and how to de-escalate the flare-up when it comes allows you to learn how to make contingency plans that cater to any flare-ups, and have tools, like helpful medication, readily available. This constant state of reflection has gotten me to a point with my symptoms when I can feel them come on, preemptively change my lifestyle, and apply different coping tools to mitigate them and keep them from ever getting too bad.

This section is one of the most versatile ones, one of the most personal for myself, and most humans. In many moments, it's *vulnerable*, and in many ways, it's *critical*. Both qualities, however, are necessary for an effective self-reflection that leads to action and moving forward with our lifetime management.

II.

'A BIG FAT PHONY'

Growing up, nothing made me quite as happy as 11 p.m. on a weeknight did. As soon as the clock struck that hour, my room would be filled with the infamous *Family Guy* theme song accompanied by my over-the-top vibrato singing along to it. As controversial as it has been (in some spheres), the *Family Guy* series has its own dedicated bank in my mind in which I've deposited hundreds of references and quotes that have stuck with me throughout the years. I quote it, to a lot of blank faces at times, and have frequent flashbacks to different episodes.

I credit this show with a lot of what my humor and storytelling has developed into. So naturally, in my biggest creative storytelling endeavor, I thought the best way to begin our "Reflect" section would be to pay tribute to something I watched in the beginning years of my life. Now, let's talk about being "a big fat phony."

In the series, the term "big fat phony" derives itself from a situation in which a provoked man calls Peter Griffin "a big fat phony." The reasoning behind it isn't relevant to our story, but the scene itself depicts how invasive the harsh words of a critic can be on the life of whoever is the subject of the criticism.

Let's face it: no matter how tough your skin is, or how "c'est la vie" your attitude toward life is, words can hurt, and knowing they come from a place of harsh judgment can get into anyone's head. Many of us become so consumed with the fear of what other people might think of us that we become paralyzed, unable to do something we really want to do. Now, for those of us who are able to persevere and accomplish our tasks, we sometimes focus so much on what other people have to say that we forget to enjoy and to celebrate our achievements.

But what about when those paralyzing thoughts and voices come from within? What if the persistent and loud accusation of being a "big fat phony" is something we're internally yelling at ourselves?

I was twenty-two when I found out that the answer to these questions had a name, and that name is impostor syndrome.

The Oxford Dictionary defines impostor syndrome as "the persistent inability to believe that one's success is deserved or has been legitimately achieved as a result of one's own efforts or skills."[46] Some of us experience this phenomenon so richly that it stops us dead in our tracks because of our fear of being unworthy of achieving our goals. We fail ourselves by never allowing ourselves the opportunity to grow.

Though impostor syndrome isn't a recognized disorder, I like to think of it as a really close friend of anxiety. Anyone

---

46 *Lexico Dictionaries powered by Oxnard*, s.v. "Impostor Syndrome (_n._)," accessed on May 8, 2020.

who experiences it can get an idea of how debilitating anxiety can be.

In my life, my anxiety of what other people think and the imagination of what "could" happen if I do something is typically what sparks feelings of being an impostor. This feeling creates a domino effect, as it triggers a depressive state and all of the impediments this state brings with it. And then, out of fear of people discovering my weaknesses and agreeing with my thoughts of being unworthy, I refuse to talk about it, and through isolation, I suffer in silence.

But despite the contrary feeling of loneliness that this isolation brings on, I'm not alone in experiencing impostor syndrome. According to research, it's estimated that 70 percent of the population suffers from at least one episode of impostor syndrome in their lives.[47] But even that estimation seems a bit low, especially considering that anxiety disorders are the most common mental disorder in the United States, affecting forty million adults every year and one in thirteen people globally.[48]

Personally, I feel like the 70 percent statistic can describe how often in my life I feel unqualified for what I seem to be tackling at any given moment. This impostor syndrome has led me to feel a lot of self-loathing that has hindered me more than I'd like to admit. I've sat at many tables where I felt like I was biting off more than I could chew. I've made myself sick in my efforts in those moments to find whatever validation I felt could prove my inferior feelings wrong. Once

---

[47] Jaruwan Sakulku, "The Impostor Phenomenon," *The Journal of Behavioral Science* (6 (1), September 2011), 75-97.

[48] "Facts & Statistics," Anxiety and Depression Association of America, ADAA, 2018.

that sickness would subside, then the self-deprecation and loathing would kick in. It's a topic that's very near and dear to my heart, but it was also my biggest barrier in deciding to write this book, thus, making it the first one I wanted to address in this section.

When I first decided on the concept of this book, I discussed it with a few close friends. With every conversation, I was more energized and in love with the idea than I was before. I loved it, I loved what it could be, and I loved what it could do for others. But as I began my research and empirical studies, I couldn't help but get riddled with that all-too-familiar anxiety. Who did I think I was writing a book on my life with depression at the tender age of twenty-two? Rental car companies barely trust me to rent a car from them, even when I pay a premium for being my age, so why would anyone want to read my self-proclaimed manifesto on how to live life with mental illness?

And with that, it became challenging to come to terms with why I should continue to do this. I wanted to stop before I even started, and I desperately wanted to find another book concept. But I failed, because I was trying to find a concept that was abstract and deidentified, hoping to come up with something that would avoid any level of public self-vulnerability. I just didn't want to be a "phony," nor did I want to face any negative reviews or words. I fell into a deep state of depression over the subject matter and avoided doing anything related to writing my book.

I continued with my daily life, and concurrently had applied for and received a promotion at my job. There were certainly things to be excited about in my life. Though the nagging thoughts of only being hired due to a speedy interview process persisted in my head, the noticeable pay increase and travel perks this promotion brought helped me stay energized for the national training coming up.

I would get to meet my counterparts, and I assumed they were all around my age with different, but similar, backgrounds. These expectations caused the reality to be quite the rude awakening: I was the youngest by over ten years, and the oldest of the group was responsible for a much larger age gap. This very fact meant that every single one of those individuals had ten or more years experience than I did, and knowing that scared me.

"I must be inferior to every single one of them," I thought to myself that first night in my hotel room.

I spent that entire week anxious to speak and feeling criticized and completely unqualified to be there. I took every bit of criticism personally, and the anxiety caused me to not perform as well as I could have. Rather than taking risks and being my authentic self when crafting the messaging for my part in training exercises, I let myself change my messaging to sound more like the others in the group. Imitating others comes off as inauthentic, and it's difficult to perform well at something when, rather than using skills you've honed, you're trying to imitate skills that you need to work on.

I left feeling like I proved my feelings of being unworthy to be true to both myself and everyone else there. Defeated, I returned to my home office and walked in feeling isolated every day. I hated that I had applied to this position, and I hated that I thought I'd enjoy the role. I missed the comfort of being really good at my old role, but most importantly, I missed feeling like I did a good job every day.

But it got exhausting, and I realized that, eventually, I'd have to stop feeling sorry for myself. If I didn't feel worthy, I was going to work my butt off to be worthy. I reminded myself of my long-term goals, and that the growth I would need to achieve them involved a lot of discomfort. I typed out my learning objectives and what I needed to do to be good in my role. I began to work on them so much that I annoyed myself with the repetition. Eventually, I received an opportunity to showcase my skills in a project, and I did it so well that it was praised by the same people who once questioned why I had the seat that I did. Especially myself.

The bright side of starting with a lower bar is that proving everyone wrong with your great performance can get you the extra title of the "most improved" award. I started being tasked with more assignments. My newfound confidence allowed me to complete these assignments more authentically, and it made others realize some skills I brought to the table that were unique in my role—analytic skills, Excel proficiency, social media skills—all of which were, in some part, because of my age. What I once viewed as a visible weakness was a valuable asset to the team. I felt unworthy because I was different, but being different is just another word for being unique.

However, seeing the unique aspect is hard in the moment because if you're unlike a lot of people around you, you're judged, and that makes you susceptible to judging yourself and experiencing impostor syndrome. It was this thought that made me realize I had positively tackled and overcome an episode of impostor syndrome, despite it having caused the onset of a strong depressive period. The motivation for this was out of sheer necessity, since not being able to overcome the issue would have probably led to my eventual unemployment. Despite that, it made me reflect on other situations this syndrome affected, and it made me revisit the episode I suffered as a result of doubting my ability to write this book.

I began to think about the topic again and the same insecurities and fears crowded my head in their loud and debilitating *Family Guy* way. Rather than ignoring them this time, I started writing down one-sentence phrases of criticisms I was giving myself. I realized these negative feelings were all coming from the voice in my head, and the voice in my head is me. I asked myself the question that helped me understand why I was doing it: What do I want?

The answer was simple: validation.

I started giving myself what I wanted by validating my inner concerns and feelings. I had a very Eminem *8 Mile* internal monologue with myself, and it went a little something like this:

You're twenty-two. The idea of writing a memoir-esque book telling people how to handle their mental illness is comical. You don't have the qualifications by any means to discuss this topic as an expert. Your research consists of a lot of Instagram posts and Google. You're going to be preaching a lot of stuff you haven't always lived by.

You're judgmental. You still have mental breakdowns, honey. You don't even have an undergrad in psychology, let alone any other qualifications, lol. You've done stupid stuff, and made a few enemies in your young little life. You ready to be on a public platform for them to roast you on?

People won't think you're funny or interesting. You barely muddle through any self-help book. You can't take your medications consistently; you think you're going to write a book?

What will your friends and family think of you openly showing the world one of your weaknesses and some of your most private moments? You're going to come off as narcissistic and crazy...and what if it sucks?

I shut her off after that. I had enough material to work with, though I definitely let that voice roast me about it on quite a few more occasions. I'm grateful to hear it from her first, because if life has taught me anything, it's that Twitter is much harsher.

Additionally, the beauty of listening to her is that, though it sometimes doesn't feel like it, your head is a safe space. You have an opportunity to have passing thoughts that aren't recorded or shared unless you want them to be. Thus, the voice that once would bring me down became my strategist. Anticipating some of the criticisms gave me an opportunity to address at least a few.

The biggest concerns she had were regarding my age, my lack of qualifications, and the personal anxiety of what everyone would think. I recognized these worries, and then I flipped the switch and wrote myself a letter of why all of these things were okay.

My age in my new role proved to be an advantage because it offered a unique perspective and a different set of skills. That's what this book offers to the world. If it worked as an advantage in my professional life, I found a new sense of confidence that it would do the same with this project, too.

Age is but a number. You're not claiming to be an expert or a doctor, or telling people to use your book instead of seeking professional health. You're simply telling others about your experience and bringing a fresh perspective to an old discussion.

You should write it, because there are a lot of people who could relate to you because they're closer to where you are in life than an older and more educated counterpart. If people think it's comical that you're writing this book, then be happy you get to start the process off by giving them a few laughs.

All the time you spend on Instagram and surfing Google makes you timely and relevant to how younger demographics consume information. You're not perfect, but you've learned from your mistakes, and your willingness to admit your faults and share what you've learned from them is relatable. When someone calls you "judgmental," direct them to this chapter as proof that you are, but your judgment includes yourself. When they say they don't think you're "funny" or "interesting," laugh and say that at least you two have something in common.

Some, more (self-proclaimed) comical responses I had to my own self-criticisms included the following:

You still have mental breakdowns, honey.

'Til death do us part, my lovely unstable mental state. We are only human, after all.

You've done stupid stuff and made a few enemies in your young little life. You ready to be on a public platform for them to roast you on?

Sure, I need some more material.

You barely muddle through any self-help book.

I have commitment issues.

You can't take your medications consistently; you think you're going to write a book?

Yeah…it's probably the lack-of-medication-induced mania talking when that statement is made.

What will your friends and family think of you openly showing the world one of your weaknesses and some of your most private moments?

If this book is successful enough for my weaknesses and private moments to be well-known facts around the world, then I'm sure I would have the means to persuade them to see the positives of the vulnerability from the weekends on the yacht I'll be able to afford.

You're going to come off as narcissistic and crazy…

Well crap, public perception is always right, so maybe I should consider a name change?

And what if it sucks?

Well then… I guess this book won't be successful enough to warrant any of the above criticisms from masses… :)

Just like that, I felt empowered and ready to apply this new strategy. Rather than ignoring and invalidating the voice in my head, I took the time to listen to her. She wanted validation for her thoughts. Though they seemed mean initially, they were the by-product of her wanting to protect me from any mean things others could say. By listening to her, I was able to anticipate criticism before I received it, and it allowed me to turn my anxious thoughts into a strategic tool. In many ways, this voice becomes my partner in new endeavors, and she pushes me to plan for things and create more robust products than someone who may not question their work the way she makes me do with mine.

In reality, all I want from this book is to help others by discussing a really important topic. If no one reads it, I can't help them. The same concept goes for the voice in my head. If I don't listen to her, how can she help me?

Impostor syndrome is something that, despite the limiting statistics, is always with you. Sometimes the volume of the thoughts it provokes are louder than at other times. If you experience it, know you're not alone, and that it stems from you believing everyone else is equally as qualified as you, which is both beautiful, because you believe the best in people, and dangerous, because you don't believe the best in yourself.

If you are watching a loved one suffer through it, don't dismiss their thoughts. Ask them why they feel they're unqualified or unworthy, and begin to address their concerns with the reality of the situation, like I did in my letter. Don't make jokes at their expense that question their worth, and let them know that you'll always be their biggest fan.

What I've come to find and make myself believe is that feeling unworthy of your accomplishments is a sign you're doing something new and something that is making you learn new things and work harder, which is a sign you're doing something right. Don't let the fear of being a "big fat phony" get in the way of that growth.

III.

THE IMPORTANCE OF CONTEXT

Let's play a little game called two truths and a lie. I'll start.
1. I have dual citizenship.
2. My dog has Peruvian ancestors.
3. I once picked up a hooker.

So, what's the lie? That I have dual citizenship. I actually never got my citizenship from my birth country, so I am solely a US citizen.

Which one probably got your attention? That I picked up a hooker. While, yes, that is indeed a truth, it's not what it seems like (and I greatly apologize to the young lady I'm referencing if she prefers another label for her profession).

This story happened about two years ago. I had been out earlier during the day for a happy hour with some friends. But on my way home, I got into a really bad phone argument with the guy I was dating at the time. During our phone fight, I ended up getting so upset that I turned the car around and told him we'd talk about this in person.

"I'm not going to bed mad over this. I'll see you in ten minutes," I said.

When I got to his house, he begrudgingly came outside and joined me in the parked car to continue our conversation. But he quickly lost his patience, leaving the car abruptly and effectively pissing me off. Naturally, the triggered reaction was me aggressively driving down the neighborhood road to get to the main street, when, all of a sudden, a girl stepped out in front of my moving car. I slammed my brakes to avoid hitting her, barely missing her. She stumbled over in her six-inch pumps and motioned for me to roll down my window.

Feeling bad, I rolled down my window to talk with her, taking her for a lonely, and now startled, drunk girl.

"Hey there, would you mind driving me down a few blocks? It's just hard to walk a few more blocks in these heels," she said.

I hesitated. "Sure," I replied. Then I chuckled and said, "It seems like the least I could do for almost running you over."

She got into my car and started to have a conversation with me, innocently enough. "How's your night going?"

"Ugh, it sucks. I just got into a fight with this guy, and I'm having a rough night. But it's really nice to have someone to talk to, so I'm honestly so happy you're here!"

Well, her response was the first red flag. "You want some weed?" I stared at her, and she continued. "I don't have any. But I know where to get it. You'll just have to buy it because I don't have cash on me."

"Uhm, I think I'm going to pass. But thank you for the offer," I replied.

I continued driving, and though I don't remember the full extent of the conversation, I do remember when she motioned for me to pull over to the gas station on the corner.

"Can you drop me off here? This is where I work," she said.

And that's when I first took my eyes off the road and looked at her in her tight, short dress, face done up, and it hit me. "You're not wearing a gas station attendant uniform."

She ignored the comment, and said, "Hope you and your boyfriend make up," before she got out of the car and walked over to the corner.

That is the story of how I picked up a hooker.

I figured this anecdote would be the perfect example to talk about something I am guilty of doing myself, and that is forgetting to ask for the context in the things I hear.

Most times, it isn't as drastic as the hooker story. But in daily conversations, things get taken out of context all the time. Maybe it's a general anxiety within our society, but many people hear one thing and tend to assume the worst. For example, one day I was at work and I was telling my coworker about how I'd spent hours cleaning my bathroom.

"Since I was on my knees a lot, they kind of hurt," I lamented.

At the same time, another one of my coworkers walked in and smirked at the comment, responding, "Oh, yeah, you spent a lot of time on your knees last night?"

I laughed. "Get'cha mind out of the gutter. I was cleaning my bathtub."

Other times, it's not just conversations that need context, reactions need context too. One of my buddies got his girlfriend flowers once, and he told me that she started crying. He initially was upset by her reaction, feeling like it was unwarranted. But when he asked her why she cried, he found out that the reason lied in the last time someone got her those flowers: it was her ex, and the occasion was him trying to soften the blow before telling her he'd been unfaithful.

One thing I've learned through life is that no one does anything because of you; they do it because of themselves. Many of the responses and actions of others are their projections of how they're feeling at any given moment. Sometimes, if you do or say things without considering the deeper meaning behind it, you can trigger not only a person's current feelings, but also any grief-inducing feelings from their past. In the case of the woman mentioned above, her past feelings of unworthiness prompted an emotional response that even she may have recognized was irrational when she was able to calm herself.

That understanding doesn't make someone's actions any easier to swallow if you're on the receiving end, but it does allow you to have a different perspective in the moment. If you recognize that someone's action, or reaction, toward you seems charged or misplaced, you can recognize that you're not the cause of it and prompt yourself to ask "why?"

By understanding their actions, rather than blaming yourself for them, you have a chance to prevent an emotional response on your end, and help someone you care about feel comfortable enough to partake in a healing discussion. Though we've touched upon this idea in many of our lessons in the "Accept" section, this chapter recognizes that, for this understanding to happen, context is necessary, and it's important to highlight.

In regard to mental illness, context is important for anyone who is in the presence of someone experiencing a symptom flare-up, or the person experiencing it themselves. If you are around a loved one who suffers from mental illness, you may be hurt by their actions at times. But if you learn to start recognizing that they are not being unkind or mean because they are bad, but rather because, at the moment, they are feeling bad, you can recognize that their actions are not your fault, and it may make you give them the benefit of the doubt that they're not always going to react this way.

Understanding their feelings can make them easier to be around. Similarly, if you are the person who is suffering from a flare-up of your mental illness, looking within yourself for the context of what may have triggered it can help you better understand your own actions and how to better manage them in the future.

But training ourselves to ask for context, and not assume the worst based on summaries we hear, is hard. It also goes against how society is training us today.

In our world, the Internet and social media are open, free, and relatively accessible, allowing many people the forum to express their opinions very quickly and very harshly, with little thought and effort required. This platform has also made all of us public figures in some way, especially those of us with active social media accounts. Without warning, without training, and without fully disclosed consent, every one of us has opened ourselves to criticism on anything we post, which becomes especially damaging when our short tweets, captions, and comments typically lack context.

Now, it is important to highlight how beneficial social media is. A bountiful platform that has opened the world and given society a chance to connect in an unprecedented way. Through social media, charities and nonprofits have a means of sharing their important work and raising critical funds, family members are able to stay in touch even when they're thousands of miles apart, businesses can affordably grow their consumer bases, and millions of talented individuals have been able to share their gifts with the world. I wouldn't choose to live a life in which social media didn't exist, because there are so many unprecedented benefits to it.

But it has a dark side.

Though the hyperconnected world we live in makes us efficient multitaskers, research implies that our use of the Internet could also translate to a thirst for instant gratification, settling for quick choices, and lacking patience, depending on how we adapt to this new environment.[49] These three qualities can explain why people tend to gravitate toward those streamlined headlines and bullet-point articles, and why asking for context is an inconvenience few of us make time for.

When these traits influence how we handle interactions with people, we judge others based on reactions and gossip that we often don't take the time to fully explore. If we did, we'd also often find that we perceive those stories differently when we delve into their context.

Think about any time you've ever had misinformation or rumors spread about you. Even if they had some basis of truth to them, you often find that they're blown out of proportion and very antagonizing when you're unable to tell "your side" of things.

We discussed the importance of making peace with failure in our lesson about accepting that we'd never be "the best." That lesson on failure was based on the failure to achieve a set goal, but failure can also mean making an isolated mistake.

A part of the human experience is to make mistakes. But without context, these mistakes transform from personal

---

49   Janna Anderson and Lee Rainie, "Millennials Will Benefit and Suffer Due to Their Hyperconnected Lives," Pew Research Center: Internet & Technology, The Pew Charitable Trusts, February 29, 2012.

regrets to the basis of (sometimes) brutal public shaming. Doing well and meaning well are two separate things, and one-liners and incomplete information become so black and white that we rarely get both of these questions—"what happened?" and "why was it done?"—answered before lashing out in judgment.

The Internet is so quick to hop on a bandwagon of sending direct death threats, "canceling" someone's existence, and completely dismissing public figures who make controversial statements or decisions that may have been misunderstood. Sometimes, these controversial statements or decisions are mistakes that were made decades ago, and in our judgment, we neglect to give the person a fair chance to respond to it and show whether or not they've progressed in their thoughts and reasoning.

Many people have a hard time learning from their mistakes and growing because of this intense criticism. Society is so critical of any wrongdoing that many people will use it as an opportunity to completely discredit you for the rest of your life. We're so scrutinized for every single mistake we make that we're terrified to own up to them. In an environment like this one, criticism can never truly be constructive, because the person receiving it cannot accept the fault that exists at its core.

You also forgot to remember who a person is when you define them by their mistakes. Though your actions are an extension of you, so is your reasoning behind them, and the lessons you learn through the process. You may have made a mistake, but you are NOT your mistake. This understanding isn't the case if everyone on the judicial floor doesn't take the time to review your case.

Think back to my hooker story. If I were to tell somebody, "Hey, I picked up a hooker," even if it was followed up by an, "by accident," the reception would be completely different than what it is when the full context of the story is explained. I meant well, and though whether or not I "did well" is questionable, my story is a naive mistake committed by me wanting to help a stranger while I was emotional. The way that the one-liner without context plays out is that it depicts me committing a crime.

Hindsight is 20/20, but it's only so clear because we know now what we didn't know then. It is a gift, and it does not give the one who has it the right to feign moral superiority.

As a society, we cannot let a few isolated incidents define a person. Actions are isolated; behavior is not. You can make a mistake, learn from it, and redefine yourself as a person, but behaviors are harder to break.

When these behaviors become a habit, they become more defining of someone's character. At that point, we can evaluate this habit and determine if that's a habit we want or accept in our lives, and then start to associate them with the person. But even if the habit is negative, we shouldn't necessarily be wishing their demise simply because we don't agree with their lifestyle.

Similarly, statements are isolated, but context is not. Context builds on your life experiences, your triggers, your relationships, and everything that leads up to every single breath you take. Thus, we cannot let statements or labels define someone; it's the context of what makes them, them, that matters in evaluating if they're a person we want in our life.

I once read a book titled *Damned Lies and Statistics: Untangling Numbers from the Media, Politicians, and Activists* by Joel Best, and the title speaks for itself. It builds on the idea that statistics can mean anything based on context. If something as finite and objective as numbers can be skewed to mean whatever the author desires, why are we allowing lack of context to affect our lives so fully and fuel a mental health crisis?

We are all public figures, and we are members of a society with a connection to each other that is unfathomable to our predecessors. Information is at our fingertips, but so is an influx of criticism from around the globe. Depending on how much you use it, you can experience different stages of social media-induced hypervigilance that can feel like anxiety, or displacement and failure compared to others.[50]

The very thing that is meant to bring us together can be what makes us feel so isolated in the presence of others. We're all becoming more and more disengaged: afraid to stand up for what we believe in, afraid to enjoy the things in life we may not deem popular, and afraid that people will take something we did out of context and ruin not only our image, but also at times our livelihood and what feels like our life. This fear leads to feelings of hopelessness and sometimes leads some to make extreme and permanent decisions, rather than enjoy the positives of what's meant to bring us together.

The demands of the world become so much higher when limitless information is available at our fingertips, and thus, we're just trying to keep up by synthesizing it all and learning a little bit about a lot of things. Worst of all, it starts becoming second nature, and we become complacent without context, causing us to perceive stories with perspectives that would be

---

[50] Shensa, Ariel, Jaime E Sidani, Mary Amanda Dew, César G Escobar-Viera, and Brian A Primack, "Social Media Use and Depression and Anxiety Symptoms: A Cluster Analysis," American Journal of Health Behavior (Volume 42, Issue 2, March 2018), 116-128.

different if we cared to delve more into them. We also tend to view things as black or white when we don't have context. Which becomes an issue in itself with the relationship many of us have with making mistakes.

Fixating on your past and lamenting mistakes that seem stupid now is unfair to yourself and prevents you from having a healthy relationship with your mistakes that allows you to learn from them. Allowing myself to look at and dissect my own mistakes helps me understand my actions more and learn how I can be better in the future. But to reflect, I have to be given the benefit of the doubt so people don't allow a lack of context to ruin their perception of me in the process.

We are all social creatures, and seeking validation and love is a natural part of the human experience. Caring what other people have to say, and whether or not they accept us, is nothing to be ashamed of. But for many of us, our image becomes everything, and when our image is stripped down to misunderstandings and misinformation, we feel powerless, which can lead to isolation, paranoia, and distrust.

By understanding the power our words have and the importance of exploring the context before passing judgments, we can train ourselves to look into the context of our decisions and frame our actions in ways that allow us to take charge of our own narrative, helping not only ourselves, but also our entire society.

IV.

SEARCHING FOR HAPPINESS

———

The taste of the buffalo sauce from the boneless wings I had just devoured was lingering on my tongue as I was driving home. Having just finished up dinner with a few friends, I was en route to the end of my night. But right before I turned onto the highway, I got caught at the last red light I'd encounter on the trip.

The street was quiet, and I realized that my playlist had ended. It was silent for a moment.

That's when a thought randomly popped up in my head. A memory, years old, triggering a feeling of worthlessness. This memory was one I'd discussed in therapy and thought I'd resolved my feelings with long ago. I didn't have any reason to think of it or become paralyzed by it, but in that moment, I was.

"Oh, fuck," I audibly groaned. Then, I started sobbing.

I never cry as loudly as I do when I'm alone and depression is hitting. The visceral nature of it is in an effort to drown out the sound of the loud and uncontrollable thoughts. It's also the last moment before a depressive episode sets in when I can't feel anything.

The thoughts spiraled.

I started thinking about every little thing that was wrong with my life. I thought about a little conversation I had with a neighbor, I thought about impending deadlines, I thought about something that was said at dinner, and I was plagued by all of it. Normal conversations and interactions became skewed in my mind in ways that were torturing me. I couldn't make the thoughts go away.

I cried for the next eight minutes until I made it home.

When I parked, I sat in my car, and the tears stopped. The numbness had set in. I lost any desire to do or feel anything, or even really be alive for the rest of the night. I sunk into my sheets, and I let the depression sea wash over me.

Depression is miserable, and it's also misunderstood.

Depression is not sadness. It's not an emotional response to grief. It is a numbness that suffocates. It's a fog that no form of optical assistance can help you see through. It is different for everyone, and it varies in levels of severity. But many sufferers share an inability to answer the question of "why" it's there or to choose to shut it off.

When it comes to depression, you just can't control it, and trying to will only lead to frustration.

Ever since I was a little kid, I've only ever had the desire "to be happy," as simple and abstract as that may seem. But my issues with depression came at a very early age.

I played a lot of video games as a kid, and I loved Pokémon and Animal Crossing. They were the places where I could let my mind fall into the youthful innocence of being curious about the world. I experienced happiness in the simplicities they offered, like getting a gym badge or finding a cool piece of furniture for my animated home.

But one day, almost suddenly, it didn't bring the same satisfaction it used to. I started getting obsessed with the next step in the games, and that's because I started projecting my feelings of the friction that came with dealing with the high expectations I had of myself in real life.

When my depression first hit, it came at me like the infamous bus that hit Regina George. Like with Regina in *Mean Girls*, it didn't change who I was; it just put me into a metaphorical neck brace with some bruises. I was still a kid with the same interests, and the same ultimate desire of happiness. The journey and my day-to-day life just became a bit more complicated.

Whether we deem it our life goal or hold it in a lower regard, we're all searching for happiness. But what I learned in my journey of struggling with trying to be happy when I had an ever-present numbness that would follow me everywhere was that, in many of those cases, I just wanted to feel something. Even if it wasn't "happiness."

So, I felt.

I suffered from so much anger growing up that I thought I'd need anger management classes. I often felt disappointment with the world. I felt true heartbreaking sadness on many occasions in my experience with grief, all of which weren't great, but they felt so much better than the numbness of depression. Allowing myself to feel these emotions may have made me an unhappy teenager, but they helped distract me from feeling the numbness.

Emotions are fuel, and I channeled them into work, school, and everything else I overpacked my days with. This method worked for a while, but then I crashed. These emotions were no longer enough to distract me from my numbness, and they became precursors to my depression the same way that happiness once was.

I knew I couldn't live like this, and though medication helped keep me stable, it wasn't enough in itself. Even though I've never been able to answer the question of "why" depression happens, I realized I'd have to try to get as close as I could to the answer to survive. For those of us who suffer from depression, the idea of facing ourselves can be scary, but it's often the only way to increase the breadth of our self-awareness enough to figure out which tools "feel right." For me to understand it better, I knew I had to let it manifest.

In the absence of feeling, I let myself feel nothing without hiding it, distracting myself from it, or suppressing it. When I would feel it come on, I'd grab a glass of wine, and I'd turn off all distractions. It would be me with a wine glass in hand, sitting in a silent room and letting the thoughts be as loud as they desired.

I'd meditate into it, and I'd let the thoughts take me on a journey. When you fight depression by suppression and distraction tactics, all you do is put a Band-Aid over a sepsis infection. In other words, it'll take you down, and the longer you wait to get professional help, the harder it is to heal.

Through my journey, I came to one realization about my depression: it was often a coping mechanism. The numbness was my mind's response to a cognitive dissonance between my expectations and reality. Though this realization couldn't fully explain the "why," and it wasn't always the reason behind the depression, it did serve as the "why" for the majority of my episodes. When I realized that, that's when everything changed for me.

The memory of me almost drowning as a kid prompted a numbness after it, and much of it had to do with how unexpected it was. Likewise, anytime things deviated from my expectations, I would find myself slipping into that numbness. It was overwhelming, but much less so than trying to understand why the world didn't always seem to fall into fitting the role that I thought it should.

Even in managing my symptoms, the depression would come from the dissonance of thinking I could cure them, rather than paying attention to the positive way the tools would make me feel, despite their inability to fully cure it. I realized I'd have to learn how to manage my expectations if I wanted to help manage my depression.

I thought back to how playing video games started to feel different as a kid and prompt my depressive episodes. I had an expectation of what it *should* feel like, and how happy it *should* make me, based on how it had up until that point. Not meeting that expectation not only triggered the numbness, but also made me stop playing them all together, which was unhealthy because it only caused me to stop doing something that made me feel something and exacerbated the numbness.

When managing expectations isn't enough to stop the onset of a numbing depression, the only way to counteract it is to feel something.

Depression is irrational. All the positivity and rational self-talk in the world won't help retrieve your emotions until you are breathing with your head above the water. I have not experienced any viable emotional help while in the trenches of it, that work.

But emotions aren't the only ways you can feel things; you can physically feel as well. This fact is what may lead people to try illicit drugs, dangerous activities that provoke an adrenaline rush, and other physical pleasures like sex addiction.

Fortunately, I've found that if you're trying to feel something in the numbness, there are safer alternatives like…

- the embrace of a long hug with someone you love
- eating a jar of Nutella by spoon in one sitting (stomach pains are still a feeling)
- going for a run
- sitting by the window and feeling the sunlight kiss your skin
- petting your dog
- stretching
- focusing on your breathing

All of these actions afford me the opportunity to feel a physical sensation in the absence of an emotional one. To find them, I just paid attention to how these things brought me joy when I wasn't depressed, and applied whichever joyful activities also included a physical sensation when I was.

Once your head is above water, you find these same sensations can help you achieve that happiness when you're able to feel again.

If you're in the presence of a loved one who's drowning, offer them your hand, not your rationality. Help them experience a physical sensation that you know makes them happy, and be patient as they slowly get back above the water's surface. Don't treat it like it's their choice, and save your advice for when they feel better.

I've found my depression has clouded my judgment and caused me to unintentionally avoid happiness in the past. But I've learned that when fighting an invisible adversary, you can't base it on thoughts and logic. We don't always *think* what's best for us, but we do *feel*. Stop repressing these feelings, and take note of what causes the ones you'd like to recreate.

Managing your expectations while searching for happiness in light of depression goes hand in hand with understanding the importance of context. After all, we can't have realistic expectations if we don't understand the true meaning and person behind a goal.

If you find yourself in a depressive state, remember to look at those notes and feel the physical part of what brings you happiness. There is nothing wrong with wanting to be happy, and the search for happiness is a worthy one.

V.

A BROKEN BONE AND THE ART OF HEALING

It's always gut-wrenching to get the text detailing something none of us want our loved ones to go through: their tale of a love gone wrong, and their burning and unexpected heartbreak.

I have my own tales to tell you, but that'll be at a later time. The inspiration for this specific piece comes from a conversation with a friend we can call Jane. I met Jane through another friend, and though I can't say that we'd had many interactions with each other, the conversations that we had over social media and text have been extremely enriching. I've become very fond of her, so I felt her pain when I messaged her one night about an unrelated project I was working on and found out that she was really struggling through something personal.

It made sense. She'd been posting a lot of Instagram stories about "losing people" and "knowing your worth." Social media presence says a lot about someone, especially when the consumer of that social media presence is an overthinker with anxiety like myself.

After some strategic questioning, I got her to share the source of her pain: the end of a two-year relationship with her now ex-boyfriend. Sadly, she disclosed that it wasn't a great relationship in general, which made her feel even worse for not being able to get over it.

"I don't want to bug people, especially when I feel like I should be doing better since it's not my first time going through it," she said.

That made me wonder: Why do so many people believe they don't deserve to acknowledge their emotional pain? Why do they believe their grieving and healing is supposed to follow some standard timeline? Just because you've been through something before, especially an emotional trauma, doesn't mean it is easier to experience from there on out.

When you deal with a mental illness, having unresolved grief can completely hinder your ability to find ways to manage your symptoms. Even for someone who doesn't suffer from mental illness, the presence of these unresolved feelings can impede your ability to have healthy relationships. Not allowing yourself or your loved ones to grieve the way they need to is a big contributor to why people develop these unresolved feelings.

When someone breaks or fractures a bone, no one asks them why they haven't healed yet. They may ask when a person expects to get their cast off, if they can sign their cast, or if they can help them carry something, but the idea of shaming them for taking longer to heal than expected is ridiculous. But this happens all the time for someone when they're getting over a heartbreak.

The bone example serves as a very good comparison to how your heart heals.

When you break a bone, is the bone still there? Yes, but it may not feel like the same bone.

Can it still function? Yes, but there may be limitations.

Are you going to be able to do the activity that caused it to break again? Maybe, but even when you get past the medical restrictions, you're sure as hell going to be cautious about putting yourself in the same situation that hurt you the first time.

Athletes who have gotten the same injury many times have to throw caution to the wind sometimes to continue their career. But when they finally reach that career-ending injury, their ability to push through is no longer there. Their thoughts are simply, "My life as I know it is over, and I will never play again."

Replace bone with "heart" and play with "love" and you have a true depiction of heartbreak.

No one ever says, "Oh, you broke that bone before, so it should be easier to heal the second time. You know what to do, right? Bones break, it's a part of life!"

Instead, they recognize that breaking a bone once can cause it to never truly heal the same way, and that fractures may be left from the first break that makes it harder to heal the second time around. Your emotional traumas, like heartbreak, are affected by the same conditions.

So, I told Jane, "Just because you've had your heart broken before doesn't mean it's easier a second, third, or fourth time around. In addition to every relationship being unique in the levels of attachment and intensity, you also deal with break-ups becoming more and more difficult as you get older."

With every heartbreak comes more inhibitions and apprehensions about love. As you age, relationships become more intertwined into your life than they were when you were younger. You become set in your group of friends as your life becomes more settled, and any upset from a breakup becomes more shattering to your support system than ever before. You mentally feel like you're getting closer and closer to the ultimate love-ending injury that ends your life as you know it and prevents you from ever loving again.

The beauty, though, is that, unlike a broken bone, your heart is the strongest part of you, and it can heal from a lot more breakage than any of your bones. You just have to let it, and accept that there is no standard timeline, which brings us to the topic of grief shaming.

Grief shaming, similar to impostor syndrome, is not a recognized disorder, but rather a phenomenon we see frequently in our lives. It is by no means a "new" idea. But also, because it is a natural phenomenon, there's very little information on it and its definition. We'll define it as a person judging someone who is grieving because they believe their grief should be expressed with a different means, timeline, and intensity.

Grief is a human condition, and if I've learned anything about being human, it's that every person's experience with it is different. No two lives are the same, no two situations have the same context, and no two people will grieve the same way. Grief shaming really makes no sense. However, I can think of many times I have been shamed for how I grieve. In all honesty, I can also think of many times when I have been the one who shamed the griever, if not verbally, then internally.

I tend to have a habit of compartmentalizing pain. I have a pretty quick tongue, with a great ability to be passive-aggressive and dish out some witty responses in a way you're going to be thinking about it for the next few days. However, if I'm hurt or emotionally affected by something, I tend to "shut down." I get quiet and I start thinking as my mind is wrapping itself around whatever trauma or unresolved feelings I'm experiencing.

Once I've processed my emotions, the repressed comic in me begins looking at the upsetting situation with a sense of cynical humor, and I complain and I rant for sometimes years to come. My compartmentalization makes me seem much calmer and less affected during the early stages of grief, and sometimes, I have a hard time empathizing with those who are more emotionally reactive than myself.

When my grandmother passed away, I cried once alone, and compartmentalized it. I hate to admit that I got annoyed with the very expressive ways other members of my family grieved, and as such, I couldn't bring myself to support them. In ways, I was shaming them for their grief, but because of the severity of the loss, I kept it to myself.

When it comes to topics we deem to be "lighter," such as a heartbreak from a rejection of a job, school, or partner, many people tend to be a lot more verbal in their beliefs on how long and how hard one should grieve. Ultimately, it brings someone to feel as if they're not entitled to grieve the way they need to; to heal.

Like with Jane, many of us have felt shamed by our grief regarding these "lighter" topics. Like with her, we may recognize that it's for the best, or really whatever else you have to tell yourself to prevent yourself from lamenting over it. But also like with Jane, it doesn't make the pain go away, and it sure as hell doesn't fix the heart that needs to mend itself back together overnight.

When I went through a similar experience to her, I didn't leave my house except to walk my dog for three days after it occurred, though thankfully I worked at a job with an understanding manager who allowed me to work remotely. When I finally left my home for the comfort of my friends, I couldn't help but to feel like a broken version of myself. When I finally got back to work, I had to leave after thirty minutes my first day back. After a few more days of working from home, I took PTO and was on a flight to Purdue University for an admitted students' weekend to distract myself.

But still, I couldn't help but feel completely unlike myself. All throughout this, I barely ate. It was a really hard time, and it wasn't getting any easier. The amount of anger I felt for the first few months was pretty freaking scary, even for my hot-headed self. But as the anger subsided, the annoyance wouldn't go away, and I was complaining, and complaining, and still at the point of writing this chapter sometimes find myself complaining.

About five months after the fact, a well-meaning friend interrupted my complaints as I was hotboxing the car we were in with them, and said, "You keep talking about this and him. You should be over this already."

I felt guilty, upset, and completely invalidated. I processed it in a moment of silence and muttered what I could at the time.

"I don't like you giving me a timeline to heal and telling me I shouldn't be talking about this. If you don't want to listen, then just tell me that, but don't make me feel inadequate and like I'm failing at getting over it."

She was taken aback, and immediately apologized. As our discussion got deeper, I realized she came from a good place of not wanting to see me suffer. Her statement was made in the desire to see my suffering end. Though it was well meaning, it was harmful, and it was grief shaming.

My heart was like a bone that broke, dealing with all of the fractures it lived with while grieving the death of a future and a life that was no longer. I felt like I failed the previous version of myself who had invested everything into that life and future, and that I was unworthy of any of it. Everyone had their criticisms, but the person who was hardest on me throughout this process was me.

When someone you love is grieving, you don't have to agree with their timeline. But if you want to see them get better, you have to absolve yourself of sharing judgments about their grieving on them. Just like no one chooses depression or mental illness, no one chooses the misery of an extended grief. The only thing you can offer is your hand and your ear as you walk alongside them in the journey.

When I grieve, it often feels more intense because of how I have to mitigate the symptoms of my mental illness concurrently with it. I'm already my own worst critic, and I don't need another one. But grief shaming makes it harder for all of us to feel comfortable in expressing ourselves the ways that we occasionally need to.

In reflecting on your grief, do what you must to resolve your feelings, because it is a heavy sand bag to carry on your back. Though grief never fully goes away, it does have less of an impact on you emotionally as you slowly shed more and more of the sand out of the bag on your back.

It makes us cautious. The fear of another sandbag on your back can be terrifying, and it can cause many of us to shield ourselves from intimacy and feelings. But the bag will get lighter, and you will get stronger if you practice the proper form and keep going. Don't let anyone tell you that's not something you deserve.

VI.

A NOTE ABOUT ACCOUNTABILITY

"There are no excuses, only reasons, and of those, we determine which ones are good or bad."

One of my former bosses would utter this lesson, without fail, anytime anyone on his team didn't meet a certain expectation of his, whether that was being late, calling out the day of, or halfheartedly completing a project. Having been a teenager at the time, I simply brushed off the phrase and tried to avoid giving him a reason to say it to me. But years later, after having more experiences working on teams and depending on people for certain outcomes, I've adopted the same mindset my former boss used to instill in us.

Like we learned in the importance of context, there are reasons behind our every action and reaction. But that doesn't mean they can justify the effect our actions have on others. We know we cannot control everything, but we can do our best to control our response and take responsibility for when we fail. Accountability, which is synonymous with responsibility, is one of the most important traits to develop as a human being.

You must take accountability to recognize when you can be better and to prosper in our society. The necessity for someone to be accountable is not exclusive to any group, as we all must learn to hold ourselves accountable to our obligations, but it does have an extra sense of importance in the life of someone with mental illness. That's because those who suffer from mental illness have a lot more reasons to not meet the expectations of the world around them.

But if you hold yourself accountable, you start to see how this mindset of accountability can sometimes help you overcome the setbacks of the symptoms, which is something I learned in high school.

It was my senior year and my classmates and I had just trudged through the trying AP examinations that consumed two weeks of our lives. Having already been admitted to a university, I now found myself using the last few weeks of the academic year to tie up loose ends. One of those loose ends involved taking the ACT exam a third time in hopes of achieving the coveted twenty-nine composite score I needed for a certain scholarship.

With our lower family income, I was able to get the registration fee for the first two attempts waived. But, ironically, both attempts produced a composite score of twenty-eight. Having come so close, my parents agreed to pay the registration fee for the third attempt, which I scheduled after the AP exams to give myself time to study. But despite planning for it and setting my alarms, an unexpected issue caused my alarm to fail to ring the morning of the exam.

"Shouldn't you be awake?" my mom asked. Those were the infamous words that jolted me to life.

I sprung up out of bed in panic, ran out of the room, grabbed her keys, and found myself on the road driving like the crazy teenager that car insurance companies base their mortgage-like premiums on. Halfway to the testing center, I realized I forgot my calculator in my haste, and the only pencils I had on me were mechanical, which risked invalidating the score because of their incompatibility with Scantrons.

My heightened stress and excessive emotions immediately triggered a panic attack that had me shaking at the wheel. I called my mom crying as I started to pull off to the side of the road.

"Mom, I can't do this," I started. I continued with my word vomit, and then she cut me off.

"You get your ass to that damn test center and take the freaking exam. Borrow a pencil if you have to, do the damn math in your head. I paid fifty dollars for this test and, God damn it, you are going to take it," she said aggressively in Serbian.

Nothing is more terrifying than an angry Slavic mother, and the fear she instilled in me was enough to shock my system out of the panic attack. I did exactly as she said and got my "happy ass" to that test center and borrowed both a pencil and a calculator.

That attempt was the attempt on which I finally got my coveted composite score of twenty-nine.

My rough morning was not an excuse to ditch the exam, and to my mother, it wasn't a good enough reason. But that little triumph began my reflections with accountability, and I began to see it as something you *can* control. I failed to wake up on time for the ACT, but the overall outcome of pushing through and achieving the score I needed was a success. One failure does not equate to total failure, which is a testament to how accountability can be powerful.

In the darker moments of mental illness symptom flare-ups, we often forget to address the accountability we owe to others. In that moment, I owed my mom the courtesy of respecting the hard-earned money she spent on my third attempt. I already took it twice, but she had enough faith in me to invest in a third attempt. The least I owed her was to take it and do my best.

It's okay to feel, and it's okay to know you may need an extra push to get through basic actions when your mind is in a dark place. But at the same time, you need to recognize that you have a responsibility to others and that there are consequences when you don't meet their expectations. There is a fine line between taking care of yourself and not taking responsibility for your actions, and that's why it's important to recognize you are accountable for finding what works best to manage your symptoms. But the idea of figuring out how to know what you need in these instances can be daunting.

Think back to our section on self-care requiring sacrifice, and how we could figure out how to mitigate the disruption of these sacrifices by listing out what our main priorities are and making decisions and behaving in ways that help further the goals on that list. It's a similar process to this one.

Think about the times you aren't able to meet the demands of a task, and ask yourself the following questions:

- Is this task a priority to you, meaning, will you have to do it again?
- If this task isn't a priority, is it something you're comfortable not doing at a future time?
- What were the obstacles that prevented your success?

- What options do you have to tackle those obstacles, and how can they be applied in future scenarios?

One very good example of this in my life is when I got extremely depressed during my final semester as an undergrad and was unable to get out of bed in the mornings frequently enough to make it to my law and economics class. I had registered for a 9:30 a.m. class, and I lived forty-five minutes away, not including the time needed to park and walk to class. I was going to bed as early as my schedule would allow, but I had no motivation to wake up in the mornings. It felt like a haze overtook me, and I kept snoozing my alarms and missed weeks of class at a time. Unfortunately, that professor wasn't a professor who was okay with frequent absences, and I had to drop the course and extend my graduation.

I don't blame that professor because I've accepted he has a right to his feelings, even if it's inconvenient for me. He felt a strict attendance policy was imperative to properly running his class, and he expected a certain level of commitment from me. I stayed in his class post-add/drop week, meaning I agreed to his terms. I should have anticipated the depressive episode and picked a later elective course or been more responsible in taking my medication, but I did neither.

I failed him, and ultimately myself, and I needed to be held accountable for my actions and extend my graduation.

Issues with accountability are as nondiscriminatory as mental illness itself. I'm not the first person to sleep through classes, bite off more than I can chew, or try to shirk my responsibilities because I've had a bad day. But having a mental illness means I'll be in a state in which I have reasons to do so more often than the average person. This fact makes it more imperative for me, and anyone else who suffers from mental illness, to work on the ability to take accountability. Because once you take accountability, you can begin to be proactive in managing your life with mental illness.

In the above scenario, I knew completing my undergraduate degree was a priority to me, and that meant I'd have to make up for this failure. When analyzing the obstacles, I recognized that it was the by-product of my depression, which I know comes in waves. I also know, from past experience, that the haze can overcome me at any time and make it debilitating to leave bed. As such, knowing this, I have to see what options I have to tackle this obstacle. One is staying consistent with my medications, and the other is exploring later class times or virtual alternatives to the elective.

For the future, I recognize I should seek out opportunities that allow me to work or study remotely to accommodate my depressive episodes. By knowing my obstacles, I know I need flexible options. This knowledge has been a driving factor in my decision to enroll in a fully online graduate program and pursue a career that allows for flexible work arrangements.

The topic of accountability and mental illness is a significant conversation in the workplace. As we've discussed, there is an internal bias for what people don't understand, and there is an erroneous public association between irresponsibility and mental illness. But the best way to dispel that misconception is through open conversation and education, and as your own most vested advocate, it's on you to initiate those tactics.

Depression and bipolar disorder (among other mental illnesses) are considered disabilities when applying to jobs. I know this fact because, of the many jobs I've applied to, I'd always been given an option to check "yes" to having a disability with these two on a list of approved conditions. Them being recognized as disabilities is an advantage because it does entitle you to reasonable accommodations if you identify as having one. But the accountability of identifying what those accommodations are, and having the appropriate conversations with your leadership and HR, are your responsibility.

The same boss who indirectly helped me frame my perception of accountability was the first one I ever felt comfortable enough with to discuss the struggles I had functioning through my depressive episodes. During these conversations, I also explained how erratic, mean, and inconsiderate I could be when I was manic.

"Knowing that, I'll try not to take some of your snarky comments to heart," he joked in response to the latter.

These conversations were critical for him to not only understand me better as a human being, but also to run his team. He was able to create contingency plans and delegate tasks if I began to get incapacitated by my depression, which allowed him to be accommodating and ensure the work still got done.

However, I had to be held accountable to advocate for myself, and people tend to be a lot more understanding when you're considerate of how your actions could affect them.

In our society, many of us are quick to shift the blame to whatever we can. It ties into our fear of owning up to our mistakes because of the crucifixion we are afraid will follow if we do. But the side effect is that so many of us have developed issues with holding ourselves accountable for our actions. This effect is even more problematic when you have so many more opportunities in which you make mistakes and fall below what's expected of you.

But when it comes to your mental illness and your relationship with accountability, you must understand you have an accountability to your responsibilities, and it takes communication and work on your part to manage others' expectations and your performance overall.

Remembering to recognize that we are not our mistakes and have a healthy relationship with criticism allows us to recognize why we failed. This acceptance is an important step to being your self-advocate because we don't know how to communicate what we need until we fail because we lacked it. Even when it seems like it's out of your control, dig deeper into the situation and assess how good the reasons really were. These kinds of revelations can be the fine line between a crappy morning and a personal success.

VII.

REFLECTIONS ON ANGER

Imagine being a diabetic stuck in the woods with only one shot of insulin on you. Out of nowhere, a stranger runs by, steals the insulin, and throws it into a nearby rose bush. Without explanation, they run away, and before you can process what just happened, you suddenly feel your blood sugar drop.

You have no choice but to jump into the rose bush and retrieve your insulin. You're angry at the stranger for putting you in this situation, and that anger gives you the adrenaline rush that helps you momentarily ignore the pain of all the thorns scraping you as you retrieve that insulin shot.

You take it, and you save yourself momentarily. But now, you're feeling the sting of all of the cuts and unsure of how to tend to your wounds. You're angry, and it's overwhelming.

Now, imagine this situation repeats itself, over and over again on an uncontrollable loop.

Dramatic? Maybe. But for those of us who deal with chronic anger issues, our unwelcome flare-ups can feel as impossible, triggering, and defeating as the situation above.

Perpetual or chronic anger is a haze. It consumes you. Things stop making sense, and when you reflect on the situation, you don't understand exactly why you behaved the way you did. Granted, an abundance of any emotion can cause those side effects, but with anger, it's different.

My friends have always joked that they don't like to make me mad. I used to wonder why that was until I started paying more attention to my actions. That's when I realized I was the most dependable person I knew—if you were depending on me laying down the law or cursing you out if you cut me off in traffic. I will admit that most times it's humorous and surprisingly well-timed. But the underlying issue is still there, and no amount of comic relief can change that.

I've struggled with anger for the majority of my life. I have also used my mental illness as a scapegoat and blamed my manic episodes for upticks in my irritability and frequency of angry outbursts. In daily life, we can only use a scapegoat so often before we're confronted with the consequences of our actions, as we just discussed in our reflections on accountability. Eventually, after enough hot-headed outbursts, I knew I needed to stop masking the problem with excuses, and start understanding how to manage it.

It felt impossible, and very much like the diabetic in the woods struggling to survive their ordeal. I started isolating myself as much as I could when I would feel like my anger was beginning to fester. This isolation prompted a lot of self-reflection.

What I learned was that the most important step to understanding your anger is to track what triggers it. Understanding your trigger can be very difficult when you're in the situation, so removing yourself from the situation is usually the best way to start analyzing the source of the anger. It's a lot easier to judge a situation and give advice when you're not the one reacting to the stimulus.

I started writing about it since, as we've seen with numerous reflections, that serves as a component of my therapy. Whenever a situation would trigger me, I'd do my best to shut down my feelings by walking away from it, writing down what happened, and creating a poem or a short story excerpt inspired by the nugget of the situation. I primarily used this strategy during my college years.

When I analyzed and reflected on a few weeks' worth of scenarios and stories, I started to see a theme. Every single time something triggered my anger, it had to do with two things: 1.) lack of control, and 2.) feeling like I was cheated. Though these feelings seemed pretty general, I started to probe more into the creative portrayals of them in the works of fiction I composed, more specifically the characters in them.

One depicted a girl losing her big brother, another was an unidentified young female describing her situation with a tyrant ruler, and another was a young woman who walked past someone unable to speak. What I realized was that every piece portrayed me as a younger person who had something taken away from her (her brother, her power, her voice), and that's when it started to make sense.

Growing up, I felt like there were a lot of things out of my control, and in many ways, I felt like I got cheated out of a lot of aspects of a normal childhood. My family and I immigrated to the United States as refugees in 2001. We had been displaced because of the bombing of the city we had been living in. Coming to America has ultimately given me all my opportunities and helped shape me into the woman that I am today, but that didn't make it any easier being thrown into a new country feeling relatively alone.

Back in our home, we had a large network of family and friends. Here, we had my aunt and her immediate family unit.

My parents started out working low-paying manufacturing jobs, and we were living life as a working-class immigrant family. It was difficult feeling poor. I felt financial stresses at a young age: bankruptcy, car repossessions, and a lot of things many of my peers didn't even understand. They actually seemed normal to me for a really long time. Regardless, it was hard to see my parents work long hours and talk about working jobs that didn't even have AC in the Florida heat and still feel like they didn't make enough to give us what we wanted.

Their odd hours and low pay made simple childhood things like modest family vacations, music lessons, after-school sports, and hanging out with friends' uncommon luxuries. In my younger, preadolescent days, I still wore the children's clothes I had worn in elementary school, and my classmates made fun of me for not wearing "trendy" clothes. They focused particularly on my lack of skinny jeans, which were all the rage at the time.

When I finally got a pair, I wore the same ones every single school day. When I got asked the question of whether I had worn the same jeans two days in a row by another student, I quickly lied and stated that I had liked them so much I bought three pairs of the same one. They bought the story and had no further questions, but I couldn't help but feel shame for being unable to ask my parents to afford more than one pair of new $40 jeans at a time.

Over time, our financial status got better. My parents worked a lot of overtime, progressed to better jobs (most of which had AC), and thankfully, we had some lucky financial breaks as a family. I discovered thrift stores and I built a collection of new clothes. Not to mention, I started working about five years ago and have been moving up in my career in ways that have afforded me a lot of luxuries. But the shame from the beginnings before these advances created so much anger in me that it had manifested into a fire that would come out over things as little as losing my parking spot when I went to get groceries.

I was angry because I felt like my entire life was a series of being judged and being cheated of the things I wanted most by those around me. It seemed like no matter what I did or how hard I worked, there was a barrier I couldn't get past.

I cried at the revelation I learned from reading my writings about anger. It brought up a lot of feelings of inadequacy and unfair treatment that I had repressed for a long time. Finally, I understood that the anger was just the way of the hurt little girl inside me trying to feel validated for all the things she felt had been stolen from her that she could never get back.

Once I understood her, I started to understand that I could validate her in healthier ways, and thus manage the relationship with anger that had seemed impossible to me. Knowing she was the source of the pain, I began to think to myself about what mattered to her the most, and what could make her feel more at peace with herself.

I treated it like the planning of a fiction novel, with her serving as my protagonist. I started to fill out worksheets about her likes, her dislikes, her favorite memories, and her biggest pain points. I created her character, and through doing so, I validated her existence. More importantly, I personified a feeling that used to feel impossible.

I began to think of her as my friend. I wondered to myself what her favorite foods and activities used to be. It may seem strange to think of your anger as a friend who you're catering to, but making it a human-like companion helped me understand it better. It's hard to deal with an abstract concept. On the other hand, it's not so hard to deal with a person.

Finally, I started to reframe how I thought of situations that would make me angry. I would reframe the action as if it were being done to the character I had created for the anger. A good example would be that same situation of having my parking spot stolen from me. When that occurred, I took a breath and acted like it had happened to her. Immediately, I became doting and protective. I felt like I saw my friend get hurt, and I started consoling her.

"It's okay. That wasn't very nice of them to do, but you have so many important things to do today that it isn't worth wasting your time and energy on," I would say.

Then, I would find another spot, promise myself a few spoons of that favorite ice cream I had in my bag of groceries, and walk her up the stairs with confidence. It was a little success, but it quickly began to translate to much more.

The ability to reframe my anger was incredibly useful when I lost someone who I had thought of as a close friend. I found out that they had only used me to further an agenda of theirs, and they had negatively talked about me to many mutual acquaintances. This realization triggered the anger because I felt like, despite my best efforts, I couldn't control the other person's actions, and the unnecessary character assault by someone I trusted made me feel cheated of what I thought to be a valuable friendship.

The old me would have started scheming my revenge and shared a few choice words with the person. Instead, I applied that same theory of deescalating the situation by removing myself and comforting myself with the same mindset.

"Sometimes, people use you, and it hurts, but letting them get to you makes them win. The only way you'll truly get revenge is to not let them know they had that effect on you, and channel yourself into your goals so that they can't help but hear about your success," I told her.

One thing I've found is that karma has a way of getting justice for you, even if the timeline may not be ideal. But fighting karma's timeline, and reacting in anger wastes energy you could use toward positive outlets. It also just makes you look bad. Besides, an obsession with vengeance often makes you worse than the act you're taking it upon yourself to atone.

It's not always easy to abide by these words of wisdom, but an active effort to do so puts you ahead of where you were yesterday dealing with your anger. A simple outline of the approach to anger I developed from my reflection on anger can be seen below:

1. Deescalate the situation by removing yourself.
2. Keep track of the situations that are causing the anger.
3. Identify themes and commonalities in the track record.
4. Create a character you can understand.
5. Find ways to appease that character in your responses.

Now that I'm on the other end and much more at peace with myself, I realize just how angry I was over everything. But as I've mentioned many times, there is no true cure for mental illness and other parts of the human experience that life presents us with, and anger is no exception.

Sometimes, big things happen that are out of my control and make me feel cheated. These big things are so overwhelming that they release the rage I forgot I had. It's almost impossible for me to even fully follow through with step one. In those moments, all I can do is try, and through the experience, I can learn a lesson that helps me prepare for the next big trigger. Having a step-by-step approach to reference, however, allows me to find the lesson in these moments much more easily than the alternative. Without this approach, I wouldn't be able to do much other than watch the fire burn.

Though it lingers, the anger and fire that defined me for the majority of my life has diminished into something manageable. Before then, the suffering could truly seem senseless, like in the looping scenario of the unfortunate diabetic. But like my mental illness, I've accepted that it is a part of me, and learned to see the good in how it could help me understand myself in ways I never had before.

VIII.

FORGIVENESS: THE DOOR THAT OPENS

Two things I have a hard time doing are forgetting and forgiving. Often, I choose to forgo learning information that can hurt me. I do this to avoid the arduous process of trying to come to terms with something I fear I cannot let go of.

What is the context behind my fear? Well, I have a painstakingly vivid memory, and many memories plague me. I still remember a girl who owes me $2 from seventh grade (if you're reading this, it's fine, I just didn't forget that you said you'd pay me back). This memory is fairly trivial, but others are certainly not. I remember times that "friends" left me on a curb when I had a blood sugar issue because they thought I was being "dramatic," or being told I wasn't enough for someone to treat me with basic human decency.

It's a heavy weight and a burden to bear, and for me, avoiding a lot of information helps reduce the intake of things I know I won't forget. But there are some things you just can't avoid, and the world has a habit of delivering these things by the swing of a spiked baseball bat that shatters through your skin and leaves you with hundreds of scars to tend to in the aftermath.

I recognize that, while I try to filter out situations that are painful for me, it doesn't always work. To move on from hard situations, I've learned that I have to practice being better at the hardest thing for me to do: forgiving.

Forgiveness may seem like weakness, and in many ways, it prompts a level of vulnerability I'm not comfortable with. It is the topic in this book that I need the most improvement on. Unlike anger, I don't have a defined means of attacking it. I do, however, recognize how important it is to let it play out on its own timeline, just like we learned in our discussions about grief.

To forgive, you must first allow yourself to feel what you need to in order to begin the process of healing. Forgiveness may very well be one of the last, if not the last, steps in your journey of healing, but it is the most important step to ensure you allow your memories to fulfill you in the most beautiful ways.

To grow, we must create a way of processing unwanted pain and unpacking painful memories in a way that paves a road to forgiveness. My road is paved by pen, and thus, I'm attaching a letter I wrote in the journey of forgiving someone who hurt me, the same person who I mentioned I struggled healing from in "A Broken Bone and the Art of Healing." I never sent this letter, but I hope that in sharing it in this chapter, I can inspire more than just one heart through its words.

· ·

Hi there.

I'm not really sure how to start this or how to address you. It's definitely been a while since we've talked.

Though it's probably for the best, it doesn't make it any less weird considering the important role you once played in my life.

It's weird to write this letter to you at the place that I'm at mentally. We haven't spoken in a long time, and I think I've finally made peace with knowing it's for the best, even though the world likes to remind me how much the memory of us is intertwined in many people's perceptions of me.

I will admit, this isn't the first letter I've written you, it's just the first one in a long while. I wrote you a lot of letters, especially in the early stages of my grief, but each of those letters was so scathing and angry that I'm not truly sure what they would have done other than hurt you.

I was scared for a long time that the anger would never subside, and no matter how many times I called you or yelled at you, it still always felt like I had something left unsaid. And well, this letter tells me that, in some ways, I still do.

It's been an exhausting journey dealing with the fallout that you left behind.

There's no point in reiterating what you put me through. Now that I'm so spent in regards to the situation, I tend to be very stoic when I explain what happened to new individuals in my life, or friends that never got the full story when it happened. But it never ceases to amaze *me how quickly I can be reminded of the feelings by other people's reactions.*

I know that the story you tell people isn't the truth of what occurred and that you spun it in ways that would make you look much better than you actually do. But I guess I find some solace in knowing that you at least have regrets about the way you acted. It reminds me that you're not a bad person, you just made some poor choices.

I went through a long journey of healing.

Your actions provoked the rage and anger I had worked so long to get under control. It took a long time to express it all and finally quell the fire. But once the rage subsided, the devastation kicked in.

I would go through episodes of uncontrollable tears that unleashed themselves in the most inconvenient situations. The worst was when they would creep up on me at work. But on the bright side, I mastered the art of silently crying in my cubicle. I even lied to coworkers that I was congested so they wouldn't question why I was sniveling so much.

It got so bad that I had to start changing aspects of my routine. I started frequenting different spots, and I always brought someone with me to events so that I wouldn't be alone. Anything that reminded me of you had to be avoided, and so came a huge inconvenience to my life of creating buffers and layers to avoid triggering the grief. This meant losing people and pleasures that I had enjoyed while we were together.

All of this caused me to say a lot of really mean things, and I couldn't help but wish a lot of really bad and negative fortunes upon you. I'd prefer not to repeat them, but it was the only thing that felt right at the time, and I couldn't keep from expressing it. But I'm sorry because I know how much that must have hurt.

When the anger started to quell, I finally began to let go. But I didn't do it all on my own. I looked to my friends for support by giving them different aspects of my pain to unpack and get rid of. It became a little easier not doing it all myself because doing it alone reminded me too much of what had occurred.

Over time, I got to a point where I stopped thinking about you as much, and the crying spells reserved themselves for sad Netflix movies. It seemed as if I had gotten to a point where I was successfully repressing my memories, and I thought that was enough.

That was, until, one day I was in the midst of a group of friends, and I threw out a one-liner in a silly accent in response to something someone said. Though it got a few light chuckles, nobody really got the joke.

That's when memories started rushing back of you, and how we never uttered that same phrase to each other without a laugh. You got my jokes. You always had. I kept the dialogue, but I lost my companion. And if I *didn't learn how to forgive the memory of my companion in my head, I'd lose that part of me.*

If I repressed you instead of forgiving you, I would be repressing the beautiful parts of the time you were in my life. I have to forgive the bad to see how you positively affected me. Otherwise, I'd be neglecting a lot of growth.

So, I reintroduced myself to you in my head. I went over how we met, deep conversations that we had, and the good moments like when you jumpstarted my car on your lunch break or carried me when I physically couldn't walk in my heels.

I let myself feel everything, and I allowed myself to recognize all of the growth from it.

There is no mistake in our universe, and everything happens for a reason (though I may argue a lot of those reasons suck). But you were no exception. Some of your actions may have hurt me, but they served me.

I went to therapy because of how unresolved I felt from our time together, and I got to express much more than just my issues with you. My therapist and I got to deal with things that I had been repressing for far longer. You were the catalyst that got me some help I really needed.

I lost friends that got tired of how angry and exhausting I was to spend time with because of how affected

I was by the fallout. I was so mad and angry over it until I realized how happy I was to have them out of my life. Funny how we forget some of their toxic traits when we're in the friendship.

I felt like you didn't know me, and that you didn't try to understand my passions and my talents. So, when you were no longer in my life, I devoted myself to those creative pursuits that being with you made me neglect.

You gave me hard lessons and taught me about myself. Now, I'm healthier for it.

The biggest thing I realized through this self-reflection is that playing the blame game doesn't help anyone involved. We all make mistakes, and they're never one-sided. We were young, and we both did things that may have been misguided. At their base, our intentions were pure. And we grew from it together.

I realized that you loved me. And though sometimes your decisions hurt me, I just hope you learned from it. I hope that my patience made you a better person.

I thank you for your lessons, I thank you for the good memories, and I thank you for loving me while I grew because I love who I grew into.

I forgive you... and in forgiving you, I hope you can respect my decision to stay connected to your spirit as I physically let you go.

I hope you have a happy life. And for the first time ever, I mean it.

Much love,

Nikolina

• •

No cure is found for processing a wrongdoing. To advise someone to not let it affect them is extremely misguided. Everything we experience turns into a memory, and those memories shape our identities and affect our lives indefinitely. To ignore them is to ignore ourselves, and, well, a flower never blooms if you don't water it.

When a door closes, we lose whatever we left behind. To get back in and grab our stuff, we must open it. Forgiveness is the tool that helps us open the door.

Forgiveness is not a solution; it's a journey, and a hell of a tool for learning how to manage our pain.

IX.

REFLECTIONS ON YOURSELF: THE OTHER HALF OF FORGIVENESS

I talk a lot through these pages about experiences and people whose actions have affected me, for better or for worse. Sometimes, those people I describe have played pretty antagonistic roles in my life. Whether or not they would agree is subjective, but it's important to understand that no interaction is a one-way street.

Each person whose story I've shared would tell it differently than I would. In their stories, maybe I'm the antagonist who reacted selfishly and did things I should not be proud of. Maybe the context explaining their actions would overshadow my interpretation of events. I recognize that, like I process my pain and have my own feelings on how a story plays out, others do so in their own narratives as well.

Processing external stimuli can be very difficult when you suffer from a mental illness. Sometimes, it can be so consuming, that you lash out and treat others in ways that drive them out of your life. It's a taxing by-product that can make everything feel worse. But if we learn to accept accountability for our actions and be considerate of other's needs, we can often fix the strains on each of those relationships.

What if there is no fix for a relationship? What if the chance to mitigate it has passed, and you must now live with the consequences?

In these instances, we've already learned that we have to accept that people will leave our lives and fighting it will do more harm than good. Now the next step in the journey of healing is to learn to forgive yourself.

I wrote another letter on the concept of forgiveness. But this time, I was soliciting it for myself.

• •

Hi,

I've cried a lot over the past few months as I've unpacked the lessons and emotional journeys that I've been through getting to a better place with my mental illness. Some feelings and memories were more difficult to relive than others, but the hardest thing I've had to do, by far, is ruminate over many of my own mistakes.

I am no stranger to taking accountability for my actions, and I want to offer anyone who needs closure the opportunity to get whatever they need from me to heal. But sometimes all we can have from a situation is a hard lesson because the damage is too far gone. In those instances, I'm the bad guy and I need to forgive myself in order to be better in the future.

In my last letter, I let someone know I forgave them for the decisions they made that negatively impacted me and caused a dissolution in the relationship between us. Now it's my chance to analyze how my decisions and actions hurt others.

I tend to have really high expectations of myself, and that can be a burden on those around me. I get stressed, I forget things, and sometimes I nap through things that people need me for due to my exhaustion.

I was asleep when, in a rare moment, a close friend needed someone to talk to about a crossroads he was at in his life. He was choosing between a career opportunity that would require a large personal sacrifice, or jumping into a lower paying field he had more passion for that would require a monetary sacrifice. He needed support to find the courage to take the road less traveled, but didn't get it from me that night.

When I woke up, he had already made the decision to accept the high-paying career opportunity, but I know he wishes he hadn't. I can't ever make up for not being there that night, and even though he's forgiven me, I haven't forgiven myself. I keep my phone sound on all throughout the night because of the anxiety that I'll miss out on helping someone who needs me, even though I have to realize that though I care deeply for others, I can't let one regret make me feel responsible for the decisions and lives of the people in my life.

Similarly, I once got so stressed over almost being fired at work that, out of desperation to feel better, I chose to forgo a special friend's twenty-first birthday celebration in order to sulk and eat sushi. She made it seem like it was fine, but I know that it hurt her since I was one of only a few that she wanted to be present that night. I allowed my own self-interest to overshadow what she wanted from me and now she's chosen to no longer be in my life. I have a hard time forgiving myself whenever I think about her. Now, I push myself to the limit and find that I strain my relationships from stretching myself too thin by never wanting to decline an invitation.

On a more trivial level, I've forgotten to bring items to potlucks and other events that I've promised to bring things to because of the stress and overloading I put upon myself, and I've thoroughly annoyed my friends and those who've depended on me. It causes me to overcompensate when I do contribute, and I always feel as if I have something to atone for long after the events have passed.

I can be very tunnel-visioned when I'm in a certain mindset. I have to recognize that my expectations, my reactions, and my emotional sensitivity are a load that I put on the people around me.

I overload myself, get stressed, and my friends are taxed to provide more emotional support in those moments. A lot of the time, I do this to myself by doing too many things that are self-imposed. No one told me to work full time, go to grad school, write a book, AND continue all of my social and voluntary commitments. I chose to do it. That doesn't mean it's okay for me to be snippy with my family members and friends who need something or expect them to be there for me if I'm having a mental breakdown from the stress.

But the mood I'm in affects their day, and it's unkind of me to put a negative one onto them. For that, I have a hard time forgiving myself. It can cause me to shut off emotionally to avoid passing on the burden of my feelings, but that can strain any type of interpersonal intimacy.

Similarly, my self-imposed daily requirements don't excuse me for being a terrible texter for weeks on end when I'm in my tunnel vision. My friends have every right to be upset with me for my delay, and as such, I have a 9:30 p.m. alarm clock every day that goes off to remind me to respond to messages (though sometimes I have to ignore that too).

I've accepted that I have a conflicting relationship with how intense I can be.

My roommate always jokes that her friends are afraid of me. In some ways, this is kind of a nice trait to have because I normally don't get pushback if I ask them to lower the volume or clean up after themselves when they visit our home. But in many ways, it's not always appropriate, and that kind of interaction can make someone feel very uncomfortable. I try to remember that and just be better, though I do have flashbacks of my unkind intensity taking over an interaction.

Why do they think I'm intense? Well, I once stood in my roommate's bathroom staring her down to finish her eyeliner because she was thirty minutes late to a concert I had given her my second ticket to. In reality, I should have just told her it started an hour earlier than it did to allow for wiggle room, but at least, in this instance, I know she still loves me.

In the heat of the moment, consumed by my own needs and desires, I can forget that other people have feelings and that my actions negatively impact them. I can hurt their feelings, hinder their mood for the day, and cause it to ripple down to others. This could take form in a joke I make at someone else's expense, or emotions being very visible on my face.

Though not frequently, I'm late to things. Sometimes it's at the fault of my own planning. Other times, it's due to the ripple effect of other situations. But regardless, I set someone off their schedule, and despite the reason, I have to take the blame for that.

Sometimes, I don't deliver what someone expected. Whether it be for work, a school project, or a promise that I made, people depend on me, and whether or not I can justify it, I let them down. Sometimes, it creates trust issues in the other person. Other times, it means that I'm forcing someone to work more to compensate for what I didn't give them. It's not always easy, and *it may mean that they have to miss their daughter's birthday or driving their mom to the airport before a big trip. A lot of the times, the reasons for this are selfish (i.e. a few extra hours of sleep for me that causes them to miss an experience they won't get back).*

My pessimism can cause me to discourage someone I love from following an idea or dream because all I can think of are reasons why it won't work.

That discouragement could be enough to keep them from following their dream. Their life becomes less fulfilling, and they become stuck in their current situation out of the fear and doubt I put into their mind.

When I forget to smile back at someone who smiles at me, I negate a little bit of positivity they were trying to share with me.

I hurt them in ways I neglect to understand in the moment, and I instill a negativity that they reflect onto everyone else they come into contact with that day.

I can argue someone's constructive criticism very defensively.

Sometimes, it discourages them from ever speaking out again, or sharing thoughts that could truly improve a process or experience, simply out of my own pride (hence why it's important to take the lesson on context and accepting personal failures seriously enough to be able to avoid something like this scenario).

I prove to be that antagonist in those people's lives.

Their stories of me in therapy, their journals, or to their friends can probably describe me by a few choice words. I have to accept that, and I owe it to them to be better.

For those of you who I've hurt, I want to take a moment to thank you for your patience and commend you for carrying the weight of my actions on your shoulders. You were worth the courtesy, smile, or accountability that I promised you, and before I ask you for forgiveness, I simply want you to know that you're worth what you asked for, and I want to make sure that you never doubt yourselves because of me or my actions.

I hope that in knowing that your interactions have prompted reflections in myself, it can bring you some sort of closure. I haven't forgotten my actions, but I don't want them to burden you in any way. I ask that you forgive them, not for me, but for yourself. May your journey lead to a place where you can remove that weight from yourself, and I am here to offer you the closure you need, even if it's more than just this realization.

And if you can't find it in your heart to forgive me, then I'll forgive myself and be a better person in your honor.

Thank you,

Nikolina

Writing that letter, though it has MANY examples, felt extremely condensed. I could go on and on about the things that I do on a daily basis that may have a negative effect on others. The takeaway is that our actions have so much power, even if we're not aware of it in the moment. But for many, like myself, they don't mean any ill will; they just get consumed in their own self-interest. But we know that taking accountability means accepting that there are consequences, even in light of no ill intent.

It can be disheartening to realize that we can quickly negatively influence other people's days or lives. But that's why forgiveness is important on both fronts. If we can forgive others, we can forgive ourselves, and not let the weight of our past regrets cause us to continue a trend of negative behavior.

When we learn to let go of this weight, we can analyze our mistakes and adjust future behavior as we've learned in previous chapters. But just like we learned in "This Too Shall Pass," it can be hard to find motivation if you feel overwhelmed by the current state. You can absolutely make a difference, and it can quickly ripple. Fortunately, through reflection and action, you can make it a positive one. It's important to pay attention to the positive little ways we affect people's lives.

It could mean sacrificing your weekend to work diligently and beyond the duties of your role at work to ensure client satisfaction, or it could mean picking up a shift you didn't want because your coworker needs to study for an exam or attend their daughter's recital, or blatantly taking the fall for others in a work situation because you have more seniority and job security than the person who made a mistake.

Little acts of kindness go a long way, and they prove how complex human beings are. In the same day we may negatively affect someone's life like in the ways I disclosed in my letter, we can also do amazing acts of kindness that save someone's business, scholarship, relationship, or livelihood. Knowing this is what makes forgiveness so powerful, because anyone who feels vilified and unforgiven will have a harder time practicing this kindness that makes our world a better place.

Whether you see the immediate impacts of it, your actions have an effect on others, and they can be good or bad depending on what they are. No one is able to ensure that every single interaction is positive, but you can make a positive impact by continually working to improve yourself.

I've talked a lot about my growth. But to grow, we all have to reflect on how we affect other people's lives, and what role we play. Once we do that, we can learn to be better, and we can move to embrace the positive while being conscious of the actions and roles we may not be proud of. This letter and chapter are an example of how this can be done that can, hopefully, serve as an inspiration for others. Once you are able to recognize the specific moments, actions, and habits you are responsible for, and the effects they have on others, it can serve as a means of evolution, rather than being.

To grow and get to a place where we embrace the negatives in our lives in a positive way, we must reflect and continuously evaluate our roles in the lives of others, and in the world itself. It could mean removing ourselves from our own perspectives. It could mean creating an intent to do a positive thing during your day, and evaluating what it was, how it went, and how people reacted to it.

Most importantly, we must understand that people have a right to their feelings and understand how we fuel those feelings through our actions. We cannot have expectations of someone that they simply cannot fulfill. We must allow others to forgive us on their own timelines, and we must forgive ourselves for our negative actions so we can grow from them.

Forgiveness is a personal decision, and it's a very vulnerable state to be in. We cannot expect it; we can only control it if we choose to apply it for ourselves. I hope you've been able to recognize the benefits of how freeing it can be and forgive those who have hurt you in any way and allow them to be better through your forgiveness. Know that you are an important part of their evolution, and you will never be insignificant. Find it in your heart to let go, so that we can all free ourselves from the weight as we reflect on what role we play in this world and work toward becoming the people we'd like to be.

I forgive those who have hurt me, and I hope they are able to move on in their journey of healing and forgive me as well.

A CONNECTION (REFLECT TO EMBRACE)

Depression and anxiety have been my unwelcome companions since I was eight years old. Being almost twenty-four now, they've been a prominent part of my life for the majority of my time on this earth.

We've taken some time to accept some truths that, though not always easy or good, can help us in managing our illnesses. We also reflected on memories and themes that have shaped how we manifest and manage our illnesses. Now before we can embrace the beauty of what can come out of a life of managing your symptoms successfully, we must once more reflect on the ugly side of mental illness.

Corinthians 15:33 has been cautioning those who study the Bible for millennia to "not be misled: bad company corrupts good character." For my dear friend sharing her story with us during this chapter, this message is something she holds closely.

This friend of mine is also one I met in college. She personally requested to be referred to as Jelly Bean Jones, which we'll shorten to JBJ.

She's a beautiful person in and out and has been there for me through many different scenarios. We've stayed close friends throughout the years. She's had a lot of success and has been able to figure out what direction she wants her life to go in, which is even more inspiring when you know some of the struggles that her mental illness has put her through in her sixteen-year journey of managing her symptoms.

They came in a few pretty standard forms. Depression was always dark, exhausting, and numbing; it was the same familiar feeling that I would sink into. Anxiety was urgent, nauseating, and violent, causing sheer panic in an array of situations that unaffected people can handle without thought. While I believe I was born with a predisposition to these issues, I did suffer through traumas that seem to be a catalyst in the severity.

These symptoms were always with her and seemed to tag team in ways that never allowed her to get a break.

For a long time, the draining feeling that often accompanies my depression kept me from doing so much. On the days when the dark clouds would part and I caught a break of sunshine, the anxiety would set in, sending tornados and thunder causing me to run for cover. It was always something; either one or the other or both, but never nothing. I don't recall a single day where negative thoughts did not plague my brain.

Like with my friend who shared his story between the "Accept" and "Reflect" sections, I didn't know that JBJ dealt with these demons when I first met her. She was always cracking jokes, she was energetic, and she was kind to everyone around her. But after some time of seeing her mannerisms and the manifestations, I began to recognize certain quirks that reminded me of my own: mood variations, dark humor, impulsiveness.

A lot of frustration for both of us came from difficulties in dealing with the diagnosis and treatment of our mental health issues. I've had to argue with psychiatrists about my diagnosis and the medications they wanted to put me on, which was exhausting even for my confrontational self. For someone who began her initial medical treatment at the tender age of sixteen, she put more faith in her medical professionals to guide her. But now, she feels they failed her because of the stigma and general view of it in the medical field.

Not only has it been difficult to escape the anxiety and depression themselves, it has been a challenge escaping those labels in the medical world. I feel like when I was diagnosed, the only two illnesses someone like me could have were either anxiety or depression, sometimes both. No effort was put into determining whether it was actually borderline personality disorder, obsessive compulsive disorder, bipolar disorder, or any other illness.

It was just anxiety and depression. The labels that have been stuck to me since I was formally diagnosed at sixteen. It's been frustrating because I feel as if I am the one responsible for bringing up other disorders with my doctors for them to explore. This has brought up other, more accurate diagnoses such as obsessive-compulsive disorder.

The difficulty of this mindset is that many of us have to go through trial periods of different medications to help our symptoms. It can be a long journey to make it work, especially when your doctor isn't giving you the proper diagnosis.

We used to joke about the side effects of our medications together. It would be light-hearted, yet dark, a very distinct comical trait of those who deal with mental illness.

"You took Seroquel, too?" she'd ask.

"Yup. Were you also knocked out for seventeen hours and felt like a train hit you when you finally woke up?" I'd reply. She'd chuckle, and then tell me a story of how the negative side effects made her miss something she needed to do.

Though we were light-hearted in our banter, we both knew the dark side of what we were dealing with. I went through a pretty bad withdrawal when I abruptly stopped my medications (something I am NOT endorsing, so do not use me as an example). But I've been able to find a way to manage my illnesses without the medications (for now). My stomach wasn't a good fit for what they gave me, so it was more out of desperation than arrogance.

When you finally do find a medication that works for you, it's incredible.

But it's not the end of the journey, as other problems can arise if life gets in the way of taking them. JBJ began taking antianxiety medication and antidepressants when she was sixteen. They've become integral in her routine and she deals with awful side effects if she misses a dosage, something she's described as "a total shutdown" of her life.

I have always been diligent in taking medication, but as we know, life sometimes gets in the way. When I was in college and didn't have a car my freshman year, I didn't always have a way to get to the pharmacy to pick up my prescriptions. Recently, my insurance randomly stopped covering my antidepressant for reasons I still have not found.

Other times, the reasons for not being able to take your medication have nothing to do with your own willpower.

During a brief hospital stay after a suicide attempt, I was not allowed my daily medication while the doctors pored over my medical history. It starts with "brain zaps." That is the most accurate term I can think of. They come thirty-six hours or so after missing a dose. Any movement of my head causes this rattling feeling, like my brain is jolting in my head, like I have miniature jumper cables on each side of my skull. My eyes take a little longer to adjust to my head's position as the electricity bounces around. I start to sweat and switch between extreme heat and shivering cold.

After the "physical" symptoms come on, then the mood shifts begin to take over.

The irritability hits next, causing me to snap at my loved ones out of frustration of the physical sensations. My mood begins to shift and I have very little control of my emotions. Tears flow for seemingly no reason as the physical effects worsen. I do not feel like myself. I am angry, confused, and nauseous. I know what is happening and I have little control over it. Sleep comes with a fight and is filled with vivid nightmares. These disturbing images keep me in a light sleep and I wake feeling like I had no sleep at all. I am drenched in sweat when I wake up, my hair matted to my neck, and my shirt soaked through.

The worst part is how weak it all makes you feel.

This is the most frustrating part of my illness because I have so little control over it. Until I am able to take my medication, I withdraw like this. It feels shameful almost because my body relies so heavily on these little pills.

In this weakness, we become desperate for any kind of "fix" or "solution" that can help us take back control of our bodies, whatever the cost may be. We become desperate, less skeptical, and more optimistic in the face of the warnings, hoping we can be an exception.

When I began taking these medications, more specifically SSRIs, I had no idea the effects they would have, I was just hoping they'd fix me. A quick Google search reveals the dark world of SSRI withdrawal. It is a living hell.

The dark side does not lie simply with the withdrawals of missing medications. A lot of it lies in the daily management of all of the complications that living with a mental illness can inflict upon someone.

Aside from withdrawal, the complications of mental illness in my daily life vary. These things truly complicate my life, making me jump through hoops just to feel some sense of normalcy. Random nihilistic and alarmist thoughts intrude when the world around me is bright. Physical exhaustion plagues me after a solid night of sleep. Panic and nausea set in when

I am not threatened. Reason eludes me when it comes to why I feel these things.

As we've discussed prior, the symptoms and manifestations of mental illness aren't static, and JBJ has noted how they've been changing for her. The past two years have shown the greatest difference for how she sees the manifestation of her issues. This dynamic nature of mental illness makes it difficult for her to be able to proactively identify and plan for some of her newer situations. It can be both physically and mentally exhausting, but for those of us who've gone through this, we find that we get better at adapting and quicker at finding ways to manage it.

For JBJ, there is a sense of resentment that sticks with her.

I cannot forgive these monsters for what they've done to me and what they've taken from me.

But overall, there's a positivity that radiates with her. Some attributed to her overall improvement, and others attributed to embracing the beauty the darkness has given her.

I will say I have improved. If you had asked me when I was eighteen if I would make it to this age, I would say there wasn't a chance. Yet, here I am, surviving somehow.

With what I've said, it may surprise some that I do, however, view parts of my mental illness in a positive light. A lot of creativity comes out of my pain and for that I am thankful. I have been able to process parts of my depression and trauma through music. While it sometimes feels like removing a

Band-Aid slowly rather than just ripping it off, it has helped me sort through a lot.

I also believe that I am now very empathetic toward others. While I may not be able to kill my own demons, I have always been very hopeful that other people can kill theirs. I don't find it hard to be positive for friends. I can always find the good in their situations and I like to try to help them see that, even if I can't do that for myself.

She's someone that has embraced the darkness, found tools that help her manage it, and found some ways to see it as a positive. Though we do not choose our demons, and we can't control them at times, we can work to embrace the abilities that overcoming their obstacles can help us hone.

EMBRACE

I.
'EMBRACE' INTRODUCTION

As Rainer Maria Rilke once said, "Don't take my demons away, because my angels may flee too."

For those of us who've spent our lives trying to "fix" our issues with mental illness, we've come to grips with the fact that it truly is a part of us. We think differently because of it, and it's here for the long haul. It's like being forced to sit next to, and work on every single project with, a coworker we can't stand at a job that we can't quit. Every time we fight with them, we get nowhere. So, we learn their mannerisms and create a strategy for how to work with them.

But what if we took it a step further?

Imagine you and that coworker go to a company happy hour and find yourselves singing along to the same song. All of a sudden, you delve into a conversation and find out you're both musicians and decide to make some time to write music together.

You do it and realize that you may not be amazing at putting together co-coordinating tasks at work, but you're an amazing pair in the studio. What was once the cause of your migraine can be a powerful muse. Your professional relationship is still mediocre at best, but the inspiration that you two give each other creatively is unmatched, and you never would have realized it had you not embraced the opportunity to collaborate.

Like an annoying coworker, your mental illness is here to stay for the foreseeable future. They're going to be difficult to work with, and at times, they're going to drive you bananas and make you wish they'd just go away. You can come up with tactics to mitigate the obstacles they throw at you, but it doesn't get rid of them.

Just like this coworker, your mental illness is more than the symptoms it makes you deal with. It has a depth to it. If you peel away the layers like an onion, you may find the sweetness within it, although it may just make you cry through the process (just like an onion).

In this section, we'll focus on some of the beneficial attributes I have developed through managing my mental illness throughout my life. By the end, I hope you harness an understanding from finding the tools and benefits it may have brought to you, or a loved one who struggles with it, too.

II.

EMBRACING THE DARK SIDE: THE BENEFIT OF COMEDY

WARNING: Please skip over this chapter if you cannot handle heavy dosages of cynicism and dry humor.

Hey folks, it's a pleasure to see you today, even though I'm not actually "seeing" you (I think that qualifies as a dad joke?). But no worries: as someone who has experience with allowing imaginary friends to accompany me all of my life, it feels pretty natural to just go with the phrase.

Welcome to the part when we talk about the beauty of having a dark sense of humor that originates from living with mental illness for your entire life. I swear, if there's one group that I can always expect a chuckle from when I talk about jumping off a cliff, it's a group of chronically depressed individuals. Heck, if you got JBJ and me in a room together, I can assure you the cliff joke would be one of the more lighthearted jokes we'd be rolling on the floor over.

So why does it seem that depressed individuals specifically tend to have a stronger affinity for humor all around (especially the dark kind)?

Well, that's because we're all so sad all the time that we figure we might as well laugh at the irony of this cruel life so we can change the breathing patterns that are typically channeled into uncontrollable sobs.

Hey, wanna hear a joke?

My life!

Ha.

My biggest hope today is that the audience of this chapter is larger than the one I anticipate for my actual comedy act. The beauty in writing it down is that I don't know if you're laughing or not, so I'm going to break off from my usually pessimistic thinking and assume you're laughing so hard you're spitting your beverage out onto some poor, unsuspecting person who found themselves in the wake of your fire due to terrible timing.

Speaking of terrible timing, remember those poorly delivered jokes we'd mentioned ruining your Friday night in the lesson on bad timing? Well, now you can ruin any night with poorly timed jokes by reading this chapter!

Did I mention that self-deprecation falls under this brand of humor we tend to have an affinity with when we're depressed? Well, that's cause our anxiety likes to say all the mean things first because we feel like it'll hurt less if you agree with us, even if you're agreeing that our jokes suck.

I hope this chapter is less awkward than the random person who jumps into your elevator and thinks they're funny when they say, "So I bet you're all wondering why I've gathered you here today." Less awkward than the car ride when I accidentally picked up a hooker who then asked me to pay for weed. Even better, less awkward than how my mother probably felt reading that chapter.

By the way, hi mom, I'm a published author. Hello beloved humans who sign my paycheck at my professional job who may have picked this book up even though I really tried to avoid marketing it on LinkedIn.

This final section of the book (and yes, I said final, there is a light at the end of this literary tunnel) is focused on looking at some examples of the good traits that can develop out of managing and living with your mental illness.

Humor, whether you think I'm funny or not, is one beautiful manifestation of some of the symptoms associated with living a life consumed by chronic depression. It felt very poetic to write it like I would write a mediocre stand-up act, and, well, if the timing is off, then unless you're listening to the audiobook version, I can pin the blame on you.

The benefits of this humor are double-sided. Not only are those who deal with mental illness more likely to engage in humor because they want to see others smile, but they're also more likely to find humor in the jokes that you, my lovely reader, share. So please thank your friend who reminds you of the dog in the meme that sips coffee while on fire but also uses the limited oxygen in their room consumed by flames to laugh at your joke.

By the way, you should probably give this friend a hug. But save the hug for the end of the day when the breakdown they may have after experiencing compassion will be able to reset after a good night of sleep.

No, I'm not talking about myself, and yes, those drops on my paper are water, not tears. Please stop asking questions.

I'm coming to the end of my set because I'm not funny enough to be a headliner and have more time, but I just wanted to leave you with this: those who are sad, don't wish it upon others (unless you tell them their dog is ugly). For those who suffer from melancholy, they may deal with it by trying to make themselves laugh, and make it easier for those around them by wanting to make them smile too.

So, smile like you're going to your ten-year high school reunion to find out that you're more successful than the mean girl who never missed a chance to call you a loser when you were sixteen. If that couldn't make you smile, hopefully knowing I'm done with this chapter of my sad attempt at humor will.

III.
DEPRESSION AND EMPATHY

—

I can be understanding to a fault. Sometimes, that means I can be an enabler because, rather than shutting down someone's negative behavior, I understand them and give them (arguably) way too many chances. But other times, it means I can be the voice of compassion for someone while they struggle.

I've always told my friends that I will never tell them to stop venting about something to me and that I could hear it seven billion times, and I'll still be intrigued and supportive and throw in a "girlllllllllll" when appropriate. That's because I understand how hard it can be to let things go, and I would never want to shame someone's grieving process. This quality is one example of it, but there is a certain breed of kindness that comes from understanding pain firsthand, and it gives you an amazing power of empathy that those without your experiences are incapable of offering.

Just like we explored how those who are sad try to make others happy in the last chapter, those who devote their lives to advocacy tend to have a story of how it personally touched them, and whether they downplay it or not, this story spurred enough pain into them to create their new purpose.

You can find this truth among the people in your life. The ones who care the most, and cater to others in selfless ways, tend to be the ones who've suffered from some type of trauma. You have to know their story and what made them who they are.

I have a good friend who some people think is "standoffish" when they first meet her. When they think "warm" and "sweet," she's probably not within the first top five people to jump into their heads. But she's someone I know I can always rely on, who takes care of others generously when she has the means, looks out for your best interest, and will find ways to help you without asking.

One time, someone said they didn't like her when they first met her because she was "mean." She simply replied, "It's the meanest people who care the most."

For someone who may not know her, that may come as a surprise. But for someone like myself who's gotten to know her closely, I know how lucky I am to have such an empathetic and amazing friend. Her "meanness" is simply a cover to protect herself from being taken advantage of. The source of her kindness and empathy is knowing what pain feels like for herself and not wanting others to go through it.

Similarly, though I've noted my intimidating nature, another two adjectives that get labeled to me by those who I'm close to are "thoughtful" and "caring." I'll share my sunblock at a midday football event because I know how much a sunburn sucks. I'll alter my sleep schedule to give my friends rides to and from the airport because I know how lonely it can feel to wait on an Uber as you see others embraced and whisked away by their loved ones. I always get a present or pay for a dinner for someone's birthday, even if it's months later, because I know how shitty it can be to feel like you're not worth a celebration on a day that should be all about you.

One of my best friends has also gone through a lot of her own trauma (we attract each other, because she's not the only one), and she's the one who'll surprise me with a wine that I made an off-handed comment about loving the very first time we hung out alone together. She's also the person who I confided that I had a bad memory of a restaurant in, so she surprised me by taking me to that same restaurant with her, even wearing the same outfit, so that I could create a new and happy memory there with her.

Then there's that beautiful person who you come to find was struggling with her own awful inner demons, who takes the time to reach out to you out of the blue after your breakup and offer support. In the midst of her own pain, she even remembers to follow up six months later to let you know how proud she is of who you've become since the ordeal.

Or it's your close friend who still considers you an important person in her life even though you two haven't gotten to hang out in over a year, simply because you understand each other's schedules and terrible texting habits, but adore each other anyways. Even better, you support each other's projects with the fullest extent (Hi, JBJ!).

It's your friend of ten years who's in a demanding PhD program but still remembers the little things about your life and cares to know all of the details of any updates. She'll also be the first to text you, "Congrats on finishing your first manuscript," and subsequently make your day.

All these amazing, caring, and empathetic friends of mine deal with mental illness, whether it is depression, anxiety, or OCD, in their own way. All of them have developed such a strong sense of empathy because they have felt pain and sadness from their symptoms.

They make you feel special, they want you to know that they care, and even though their delivery may not always be perfect (because living life with the symptoms can get in the way of perfect timing), they are loyal and always want to be there, simply because they never want you to feel the same way they have in the past.

They recognize it's a lot easier to hate someone than it is to understand them. That's because they've experienced it in their own lives. As someone who's been hated because of a misunderstanding, they'll go the extra mile to at least try to comprehend. Their compassion is unmatched, and it never would have gotten there if they hadn't spent a good portion of their lives struggling to get some compassion and empathy from others in their own lives.

Those of us who live with mental illnesses can attest that it is one of the things that makes us so caring, empathetic, and determined to better ourselves (mostly out of self-hate, but hey, we take what we can get). This kindness and empathy are two of our greatest universal strengths.

When we recognize the good qualities our illness can bring us, we're present in who we are. We want to change the negatives in the world and show kindness to those who need it the most and get it the least.

IV.

THE ANXIOUS CREATIVE

―

The "tortured" artist is a stereotype of what seems to be a tale as old as time. Whether it is historical artists like Van Gogh, who mutilated himself in his torment, or more recent cases like Robin Williams, who brought joy to others on stage as a means of taking away from his battle with chronic depression, the idea that those who suffer from a mental illness are likely to be artistic isn't new. It's still important to recognize how creativity is a relevant tool you can embrace as one good side effect of your mental illness.

I've often referred to mental illness as, in one form, an excess of emotions. Many people who suffer from symptoms typically need an outlet. Art proves to be that for some of us, but it isn't limited to what we traditionally see as art (i.e. painting, drawing, writing, music). Art can also be found in math, science, and all of those topics you don't associate with it. Art is found in the process of creation, and the true skill that those who suffer from mental illness develop is their creativity.

Creativity in the form of an art has been a common and highly effective means of channeling the excessive emotions that many of us who suffer from mental illness have. But the most beneficial way I've seen it take form in my life is through the creative way my mind is able to loop in a million solutions, thoughts, and ideas within a few seconds of engaging in a conversation. I see this creativity as a wonderful skill I've developed from my years of dealing with my symptoms.

I've been writing all my life, and on the surface level, I've viewed it as an outlet to the negative thoughts in my mind. I was trying to process those thoughts in ways my mind couldn't understand at the time, and, as this book shows, it's how I've made sense of the pain. I write letters, stories, and much more to serve as a form of my therapy. I've always known it was a way of channeling my depression.

But what I didn't understand was how much my anxiety played into that creativity until recently. Thinking about the worst possible solution because of your depression is creative, but thinking of thirty possible negative realities within a millisecond of hearing ominous news is a very interesting means of creating neuropathways in your brain to think of multiple solutions.

I saw a quote today that said, "My brain has too many tabs open." I'm sure my fellow anxious readers can relate when I say that never have I ever related to a statement more. But it was also a really good comparison to what the mind of an anxious person looks like. Think of it, quite literally, like a Google search engine. You know how you can put in an unfinished phrase and get a drop-down list of ideas to finish the sentence? That's what it's like when you tell an anxious person one bit of information and make them wait for more.

My boss could stop by my desk and ask, "Hey, can I talk to you for a second?"

Before she's even had a chance to catch her breath after "second" my drop-down has already filled itself out.

...about...
an email I forgot to proof
a project I got involved in without permission
a use of too many "uhms" during my most recent finalist presentation
too much Starbucks on my expense report
complaining about my coworkers not knowing how to use Outlook too loudly

The list goes on. The poor woman could be giving me news of a bonus, and I've already thought of enough bad possibilities that I've prompted myself into needing to take a "nervous shit."

I get so mad at my friends when they don't fully disclose things with me or make me wait because then this lasts way longer than the interlude of "second" and "about" in the above conversation. But it is such a powerful tool when you look at it as a positive (when you can of course, and when you're not stuck on the toilet because of it).

There is only one better engine for strumming up ideas from a few key words than Google, and that is the mind of the anxious creative. I've already mentioned how my depression made me more empathetic, which in turn makes me more in tune with others and a better listener. So, when someone, whether it be personally, academically, or professionally, poses a problem to me, I've already strummed up a drop-down of potential solutions before they've even finished.

I was doing an assignment for class where we were asked to strategically "reframe" the messaging of bankers bonuses a few years after the 2008 recession. I noticed that when I read the board, so many people focused on how we couldn't do that, and they agreed it wasn't fair to the public for the bonuses to be distributed. They approached it logically. But within ten seconds, I had already had my dropdown.

- *Focus on the percentages of the bonus pre- vs. post-recession. If they're less, frame it as a "lesson learned on limitations."*
- *State that bonuses took job creation and economy recovery into consideration for each banker.*
- *Quickly create a fund where x percent of each bonus goes into funding a charity of the banker's choice.*

My list went on.

It proved to be a good reminder for myself on the power of thinking like an anxious person when asked to find different and new approaches to a problem.

Those of us who suffer from anxiety freak out and get extremely anxious if we have to wait for something, and that's simply because we have time to think. Our thoughts can be extremely overwhelming, but they're different, and different perspectives are what fuel progress and innovation.

Being creative doesn't always mean painting or creating a traditional medium of art. It can be applied to any discipline you find your talent in, and these different perspectives can make you extremely creative and tactical. You just have to learn to embrace them.

V.

OCD AND GREAT WORK

"Shoot for the moon. Even if you miss, you'll land among the stars." This quote from Norman Vincent Peale is a saying I've grown up hearing, and it simply means that if you're aiming for overachievement, you'll provide something between that and the standards of what the task is asking for.

I've been a perfectionist in my work all my life, and it's led me to be obsessed with delivering quality work. The intensity behind the obsession has varied, but it's a mixture of OCD and anxiety. I become so consumed by my impostor syndrome and believing I am not worthy of something that I think about it exhaustively and make myself go beyond what is asked of me in the parameters of the assignment. The funny part is that in my preparation, my anxiety kicks in, and I believe everyone is doing exactly what I'm doing, and I keep adding onto my work until the last minute.

When I went into my interview for my current position, I spent three days preparing, and I came in with seven pages of handwritten notes on any possible topic that may come up based on a line-by-line analysis of the job description I was given (which I annotated). I also had ten very specific questions on technical products that my research brought up to me. Even in writing this paragraph, I changed the format of the "10" in the last sentence three times because I wanted my representation of numerals in this paragraph to be consistent.

In regard to my interview, I was told that they have never seen someone prepare so much for an interview. But in my mind, everyone did that, and I was going to come off as an unprepared slacker because I didn't have more than seven pages.

How consumed I get with my work is insane. The craziest part for me is that I rarely feel like it achieves the standards and vision I had in my head (the moon), but the positive reactions and surprise by those who receive it (the stars) reminds me that maybe I'm a little hard on myself.

I've suffered from a lot of stress and anxiety related to my work, and it's manifested into full-blown OCD surrounding certain projects. It's been such an asset to me that's paired with my ability to think outside of the box because of my anxiety, that I don't know where I'd be without it. This trait is a positive in my life that, though annoying, I am so grateful for and embrace (I just wish I'd sleep more sometimes).

Especially in work, my excessive attention to what I produce, as well as what others task me with to review, has saved a lot of misinformation from going out to people and has helped us avoid some difficult situations. I even got the nickname "Eagle Eye" in my office for a period of time, though the downside is that this perception did lead to people not sending me things for fear of receiving back thirty-plus notes on a two-page paper.

My creative overachiever felt like the only way to truly illustrate what it's like to live and work with this unique skill, and show how it can be an asset, would be to share a (slightly) deidentified email I sent the other day, with some notes on the actual process of sending the email.

FEBRUARY, 2020
I'm getting a shot of espresso from Starbucks in the airport to try and fuel some productivity in me when my Apple Watch pings. The control freak in me has to be alerted the second a work email comes in so I can begin formulating my response.

```
Hi Nikolina,

Just wanted to see if you could send over
your bio. Also, I'm attaching the document
it's going to go in. Would you mind looking
it over and share your thoughts? Sooner would
be better than later.
```

"*I wonder how long his attachment is,*" I think to myself.

I grab my cell phone from my pocket and pull up my Outlook email. I opened the document and saw that it was forty pages.

"*Well, he said soon, so I could realistically send it to him tomorrow and I'm sure he'd be fine with it. And maybe I should just put focus onto parts that mention my role.*"

There is a quick pause.

"*That sounds like an awful idea. I'm going to get this done within the next hour and I'll read through the entire forty-page document because there is no other feasible option.*"

I sit down, and begin reading, keeping a running list.

Hi there,

Thank you so much for reaching out! I've taken a few moments to quickly look over the document, and I have a few notes as seen below.

Pg. 4: I also noticed that on bullet 6, "plausible" is not capitalized. Not a big deal, but would be good to change for consistency, just in case the end-user pays attention to those kinds of things.

Pg. 4: Again, I think this is correct, but if we added the sentence that I highlighted in red, it would really help the message.

Pg. 4: I noticed that you're also specifically highlighting this product. Is that because the client already has it, or has expressed interest in it? I'm happy to touch upon it, but we also have a lot of different offerings that we can include, just to ensure that we're not limiting ourselves. :)

"Dear God, can I please get off of page four?" I think to myself.

My prayers are answered.

> Pg. 5: I noticed that you put these two products under the second category. They technically could be put under there, and I'm completely okay if you choose to put them there, but they do fall under category one typically.

I'll spare you the specifics of the review of the next thirty-four pages, especially the ones that were actually discussing elements of my role, but it was of a similar nature. When I finished up, I wrapped up the email.

> Thank you for your patience! Like I mentioned, this is a quick review, but I hope my input is helpful! :) Please let me know if you have any other questions, and I'll be happy to give it another review if you'd like me to.

I sent it within two hours of receiving the initial email and thanked him for his patience in my forty-page document review.

Honestly, reading this back to myself, I realize how erratic I come off sometimes, and why I get labeled "intense" by the people in my life.

The document itself was very good; I just wanted it to be even better because of my fear of letting anything slip by me. I definitely projected those insecurities of mine on the poor man receiving this lengthy email, and I can say he hasn't responded to me. Maybe that's because he's still incorporating some of my edits...

Though it might occasionally be a nuisance, and sometimes I do have to remind myself to prioritize health and sleep, I recognize the success my work ethic and OCD have brought me. This obsession with delivering good work has been critical for me in advancing my career and proving myself against many obstacles. It's not always easy to embrace something that feels like a burden, especially when it culminates in these terrifyingly long emails, but when you learn how to, it can help you find your place among the stars.

VI.

SHUTTING DOWN AND PATIENCE

I once called Apple Support because my new MacBook abruptly stopped playing sound through its speakers. I didn't try turning it off because I had a bunch of open tabs I was using to navigate through an essay I was trying to write for a class. It would have been an inconvenience, and I was hoping to hear an answer that would fix it without having to shut it down.

It may not have been the answer that I wanted, but the only one they gave me before deciding if they would escalate the concern was this: "Shut it down and turn it back on again."

I groaned at the task and obliged, quickly fixing my technical issue. I've always hated how simple, yet effective, this technical advice was. That's mostly because of how inconvenient it can be to be forced to shut down.

Over the years, I've reluctantly had my subconscious apply this same method in dealing with emotional issues. When something affects me emotionally, I, uncontrollably, shut down. The phenomenon mirrors the experience of a

MacBook shutting down. Internally, my mind goes blank and I stop processing what's going on around me. Externally, I physically look the same, but I'm not making any sounds.

Just like in the case of my MacBook, shutting down emotionally interrupts my workflow and daily function. It's annoying, and sometimes, it comes off as rudeness to the people in my presence when I abruptly stop speaking and I'm momentarily unresponsive. In the midst of an argument, this shutdown can be really challenging, as my lack of response in the heat of the moment tends to frustrate the other person.

But I've also come to see it as an advantage.

When I'm forced to shut down, I can't act or react. I just take whatever is happening around me as my system processes the issue and reboots. If I had to guess why this shutdown happens, I'd attribute it to my heightened sensitivity. I feel A LOT. I can be hurt pretty easily, and I can get really defensive over little things, though this experience tends to be true for a lot of people.

When something larger than a critique on a PowerPoint or constructive criticism on a presentation occurs, it can be totally overwhelming. Imagine being told a week and a half before a cross-country move you've been anxiously awaiting that it's no longer happening, or that you have to pull the plug on a loved one who's been unconscious for three days.

If you ask me to imagine it, I won't respond. I get quiet, I process, and I think. I shut down.

Once I've powered back on, I've compartmentalized the issue and am operating. Sometimes for weeks, I act like the issue never existed to keep from breaking down again. This compartmentalization can be hard on me, as I typically take longer to process grief and deal with seemingly random outbursts. Similarly, if you consistently restart your computer without diving deeper and finding a more specific solution to a recurring problem, you may have a hard time keeping the issue from reoccurring.

In less serious situations, I also find myself emotionally shutting down with certain confrontations. I'm typically very good with accepting confrontation and I can handle it very well, but when it affects me emotionally, that's when the shutdown is triggered.

If I'm being unfairly criticized, or dealing with someone ruining an experience for me by causing a scene, I tend to shut down. This shutdown can be difficult for me in processing the situation because I often regret not defending myself or saying more when it occurred.

A former friend of mine once started making a scene at my birthday dinner and insulting the people at the table, openly making comments about my friendships with others and putting down everyone else's presents saying, "I'm sorry, but all of your presents suck compared to mine."

It was upsetting to feel like she prioritized the attention she was trying to receive enough that it effectively ruined a special night for me. That made me shut down, ignore her, and avoid giving her too much of that attention she was so desperate for. Her behavior was unacceptable, and in some ways, I regretted not saying more to her.

I've come to find that it's easier to regret the things you've said or done rather than the things you haven't. You can typically follow-up with your feelings to a situation and find ways to get a resolution if you so choose, but you can't take hurtful words or inappropriate actions back. So, this mechanism of being forced to shut down turns out to be a blessing and a great defense against an issue escalating.

The most important thing that comes out of it is the skill of patience. After the ordeal of my birthday dinner, my other friends commented about how much patience I had with her, and that they didn't know how I did it. But they also respected me for it, and I came out the bigger person in their eyes.

I've had a lot of people say similar things to me over the years about my heightened sense of patience. I've had relationships in which I've shut down at hurtful names and comments that the other person said toward me. After I came to, I was able to be level-headed in my response, and in some ways, prompt more understanding and kinder behavior from the person thereafter.

To me, in the moment, maybe I felt like my response was inadequate, or that I didn't stand up for myself. But to everyone around me, I was calm, collected, and patient. My flaw of shutting down proved to be a skill that allowed me to control any quick and irrational reaction that others may have had when triggered by inappropriate behavior. It may have frustrated me in the moment or shortly after the fact, but it provided a sigh of relief when I realized that I didn't escalate the issue.

This habit of shutting down is not always effective, and it's not controllable. But when I embrace it, I realize that, though not always ideal, it can save me and my quick temper from causing a difficult situation to become even worse. It buys me the time to process my emotions, and when I embrace it, I realize that it teaches me the important skill of patience.

I think we've all heard the statement, "If you don't have anything nice to say, don't say it at all," numerous times throughout our lives. When I think about my opening anecdote with the laptop, I realize that maybe that laptop was following that advice.

Embracing my emotional shutdowns as a fail-safe that abides by this motto is a powerful way of viewing what is otherwise an inconvenience. Moments like the one with Apple's tech support serve as parallels that allow me to see the benefits of what my emotional coping mechanisms and symptoms can keep me from doing. In the moment, I groan, and I lose my ability to do what I can. But when I power back on, I realize that the issues that prompted the shutdown are sometimes gone by the time I awaken after the reset.

As we've learned in many of our chapters, sometimes we can't see the positive or think rationally in the moment. So, breathe, and then embrace the world you see on the other end.

VII.

(FAUX BUT) FEARLESS

I used to always joke that there'd be a longer line of people wanting to adopt Daisey if I died than the actual number of attendees at my funeral (see notes on dark humor). This joke typically can get a wide array of reactions from people. Some laugh, some exude pity, and others vocalize concerns about my mental well-being.

But deeper than the joke is, the lighthearted candor I can have about finite things that scare a lot of us, like death, especially when it's ours. Now, I don't plan on dying anytime soon (and most people don't), but I have resolved feelings with the idea of death in my head. That's because dealing with my symptoms my entire life has made me realize that nothing lasts forever, and that life goes on in the face of one fatality, and I find comfort in that.

When you suffer from a lot of losses and deal with the grief following them, you can start to become anxious that you'll experience it again in everything new you do. However, this anxiety can mean that you have very realistic expectations, and them manifesting is a validation to you, rather than the destruction of your worldview. You start to come off as fearless, even if it's not actually the case. What gets us through life is faking it until we make it.

Our faux fearlessness in the face of an end gives us an advantage because we start to fear difficult confrontations less, since our pessimistic minds assume it all must come to an end anyway. This perspective, in turn, makes us go-getters who will go where others won't, even if we wouldn't see it as a positive. We're so hypersensitive to these issues that we're willing to acknowledge the problem and make it better for others.

I've applied this ideology a lot in work scenarios. Knowing that everything has an end makes me a little less scared of repercussions, so I end up playing in the gray area and voicing my discontent more than most people (though I've gotten more strategic about it through experience). It pushes me to do whatever is necessary and doesn't allow the fear of losing something or being considered "rude" to allow me to be taken advantage of.

For many who suffer from mental illness, they may have heard that they will "never be able to hold down a job" because of the stigma that many people hold against those with mental illness. For millennials, unrelated to mental illness, they also may run into the stereotype of being called "job hoppers." Coming to terms with being in both demographics has made me feel like this faux fearlessness of mine was misguided.

These labels and stigma for someone who switches their jobs a lot is wrong IF you have the right reasons.

A lot of this stigma is presented by the inconvenience of an employer having to go through the process of recruiting, training, and retaining another employer once you leave.

They deem you "selfish" and "entitled" because of the inconvenience to them.

You know what I say to them? I have a right to my feelings, even if it's inconvenient for you.

Many people stay in jobs and roles that they're unhappy in simply because of fear of the unknown. But for someone who suffers from mental illness, little daily annoyances are amplified, and they are more unbearable than they are a nuisance. The stress from this friction may not always be seen at work, and, sometimes it negatively impacts your mood and outlook on the rest of your life. The sheer desperation of getting rid of this unbearable situation is what pushes that person to be fearless in their approach for a solution. You WANT to make it better.

But when you try, and you can't, you can justify why you want to make a change.

When will you know if it's the right change? Think back to our chapter on searching for happiness. We learned that we must identify what feels right, define it, and pursue it. The same concept goes for embracing the "faux fearlessness" that mental illness can instill into you.

I had a boss once who ended up responding to this habit of mine very poorly. Everyone in my position was miserable, but I was the only one who cared so little about losing the job in those miserable moments that I would be extremely vocal about our workload and complications in team meetings. This boss took these comments in a way that made her extra critical of all of my work, and in many ways, targeted me.

So, I started looking for other jobs, something that my other coworkers were a little slower to do than me. That's because my excess of those miserable emotions made it so unbearable for me to be in a situation like that that I started scrolling through LinkedIn and sending out what felt like more applications than there were minutes in the day.

This response caused me to make a move that's been instrumental in my growth and career progression and has led me to the position I'm in today. I also know how much longer I have to professionally work before standard retirement (a glorious forty-two years by those estimations), but I'm not afraid of anything that they can throw at me, although I may be a little anxious.

My symptoms triggered unbearable depressive and anxious episodes in my former role. Had I not had those, I don't think I would have ever had the courage to branch out and find the wonderful opportunity and amazing leadership I have now. It's also been the driver of my lesson on being able to leave the unhealthy relationships that I learned in our "Accept" section.

In reviewing this concept, I'd like to look at it like a logical chart (it's my analytic brain).

Experience in Loss -> Comfort in knowing everything ends -> Not being afraid of losing things

Building on this flow with the example of my career, I've gotten to a point that I joke about how I have commitment issues when it comes to my job. But it's true. I know that no job lasts forever, and my ability to recognize that is why I'm always channeling my work and projects into developing universal skills that could take me anywhere.

Not only does this sense of faux fearlessness push me to prepare for and expect the worst, but also the excess emotions of misery I feel push me to not commit to miserable situations. These two responses combined are why I've progressed quickly in my career and will contribute to my journey as I continue to do so (also I'm a hard worker, but that was already established when we discussed the OCD).

It's all about channeling what you view as a negative into a productive perspective, and my experience with loss has made me into the fluid (and also intense) person I am as I always anticipate it, allowing me to always plan for the next step professionally, even before the opportunity presents itself.

VIII.

BEING YOUR OWN BEST FRIEND

In a life in which you push everyone away, you learn one thing: the one person you can't get rid of is yourself.

You become your own sense of stability because you are the one thing that will never go away. You are you, and you always have your own best interests at heart. It's what makes you your own greatest companion.

Throughout the revelations of this book, I've chronicled my journeys and methods in getting my mental illness under control. I've also talked about how and why I've recognized a need to improve, what I did about it, and highlighted the importance of "wanting to be better for yourself" as the most important step to symptom management. This self-care is necessary because, though I adore my friends and family and wouldn't be anything without them, they also have their own lives.

Great friendships and relationships are irreplaceable. The people in your life love you, care for you, and support you in more ways than you can ever truly grasp. They are amazing and kind, but they also have lives plagued with responsibilities and issues you are independent of. Though they may want to be, they're not always going to be able to be there for you, and that's okay. Not only because healthy boundaries are important and constitute a basis for healthy relationships, but also because I am always with myself, and I, despite her imperfections, love her.

I've made jokes about imaginary friends that I had as a kid, but I truly did have a lot of them. It's probably a by-product of the heightened sense of creativity and constant development of characters in my head I make as a natural writer. But really, these characters are all just manifestations of my inner mind.

I didn't realize how important it is to have a good relationship with yourself until I suffered one of the loneliest and worst times mentally I've ever had.

A few years ago, I was overly involved in school (not much has changed). As such, I got involved in an organization that had a lot of underlying turmoil and politics, although I didn't know it at the time. I was very good at doing what it required of me and, as such, I moved into an executive board position.

I didn't realize how many enemies that would make.

The next six months were awful. I felt constantly targeted by people, talked poorly about, lied about to strangers, and unsure of if I ever wanted to have any kind of position of power again. I was in a really bad place. I stopped taking my medication, I wasn't working out, and I was just (barely) existing.

It felt like no one wanted me to succeed, even though I had plenty of friends who did. But slowly, my own perspective overtook the reality of the situation and caused me to push everyone away, and the lack of friends and support was causing me to go under.

Having to drop a class and extend my graduation jolted some type of response from inside of me. I was doing exactly what it felt like everyone wanted me to be doing: failing.

That's when I had to sit myself down and have a talk with her.

I remember looking into the mirror and feeling sad. I didn't hate what I saw, I just felt bad for her. I told her that her feelings were valid and getting her back to where she belonged was my one and only priority.

I had to be the one to show myself compassion in that field of loneliness and I proved to be my own best friend.

Throughout my life, I've only had my own best intentions at heart. I've recognized areas to improve in, I've been the catalyst for my own change, and I've been the one who took care of myself when no one else could.

If you've ever taken a spin class with a super pumped instructor, my inner voice has become like that.

"Yes, m'lady."

"You got this."

"Feel the burn! Oh yes! Oh yes!"

"You did it! Now, let's get up another hill!"

This encouragement has been especially important for those moments when I've been struggling, and she's been the only one to say what I needed to hear the most.

Like a best friend, she's the one who won't always sugarcoat things. So, when she sees I'm in a place where I need to change something, she's the one who shows me the compassion and holds my hand along the uphill journey.

In the case of my lonely state, she's the one who made me jump back on medications, exercise, and process the paperwork to still be able to graduate a semester later, which made it even sweeter having her by my side as I walked that stage.

Through your depression and all the other symptoms of mental disorders, you come to realize that no one will pay attention to you like you do, and no one else is as invested in your healing and progression like you are. You are your own best friend, and that's something a lot of people tend to look down upon, or forget.

Make peace with who you are, and work within the bounds of your personality. You'll never be another person, and there are some fundamentals you can't change. But you'll love yourself anyway and always be there for you.

A CONNECTION (WITH YOU)

I didn't think I'd get here.

When I started writing this book, I didn't think I'd get here. When I was in high school, I didn't think I'd get to college. When I was alone, I didn't think I'd ever be comfortable in the company of others. When I was miserable in unfitting work conditions, I didn't think it'd ever get better.

Even more seriously, there were times I was so depressed and low that I didn't think I'd get through it, and I'm not alone. I've had many friends tell me that they didn't think they'd "get here," and they meant having the will to stay alive, and following through with it. They didn't think it'd get better.

But it did, and it does.

Every "connection" piece we've had in this book has focused on a theme of getting us to the next section, and now that our time together is coming to an end, my focus is to move on with you to the next "section" of your life.

One thing I've learned through the therapeutic experience of writing this book is how to have a relationship with my past, while being present on my journey to the future. Every little thing has made me who I am. Not all of it was pleasant, but it's shaped me, and put me together when I've fallen apart.

If I could go back, there may be some things I wish I could have learned in more pleasant ways, but I wouldn't trade the lessons; I'd only ask for more of them.

As you continue on with your life, I have a few more words for you that I want you to remember anytime you doubt yourself.

You deserve everything with full parity. You are more than your mental illness, just like you're more than any physical ailments you may carry with you.

You have a gift in your unique perspective, even if it seems a little inconvenient at times. It's like a gift card you have to drive fifty miles to use. It'll still provide you with the joy of using it, you just have to go a little out of your way for it.

Your feelings are valid. Recognize it, and know you are worth asking for support and seeking professional help when you need it.

You can achieve anything that anyone else can. Just like you can enjoy all of the amazing moments in life: love, success, happiness. You just have to believe you deserve it first.

And you do.

Let these lessons and reflections prompt your own, and may you live a wonderful life that I hope I get to hear about one day.

More than anything, thank you for being a part of this journey.

ACKNOWLEDGMENTS

The journey of creating this book from the initial concept of "Depression as a Tool" into the beautifully bound "Outside of Your Head" spanned over the course of one year. I want to express gratitude to all of the people who directly supported the production of this book.

First, I'd like to thank Eric Koester for finding me on LinkedIn in the summer of 2019 and offering me the opportunity to write a book and reignite a dream I had given up on. You changed my perspective and, arguably, my life, and offered invaluable feedback to guide the core concept of this book.

Next, I'd like to thank my family, especially the members of it who supported the book in its early campaigning stages. Thank you...

- Irena Oljaca (Mom) for being my number one supporter, in the book and in life
- Dragan Kosanovic (Dad) for supporting my dreams and being patient with my crazy schedule for over a year
- Majda Boyer (aunt) for getting one of the first copies and always hyping me up

- Adi Rakanovic (cousin) for growing up with me and always supporting me
- Jelena Boyer (cousin) for being my (former) roommate, friend, and partner in crime

Thank you to my two beloved interviewees who shared their stories and allowed their pain to serve a role in helping others who live with mental illness.

Thank you to all of my editors who helped make this book one I'm proud to share with the world. Specifically, thank you to Karina Agbisit, who worked to develop my stories into a structured manuscript, and to Kristy Carter for taking that first manuscript to a whole 'nother level (and making me laugh through revision-induced tears with your witty comments).

Thank you to the beta readers who took on an editorial role in providing early feedback to help enhance the book before copy editing:

- Francesca Rivera
- Brice Pinson
- Sebastian Parker
- Justin Rodriguez
- Omar Altoubah
- Jade Rohn
- Anneliese Long
- Angelina Lovalente
- Kara Senesi
- Vinh Dinh
- Andres Rodriguez
- Lissette Deza
- Samantha Simcox

- Stephanie Wheeler
- Lauren Daniels
- Oliver Varah
- Michelle Adams
- Nikolas Jen
- Alliyah Edwards
- Maricarmen Garcia-Ramos
- Dante Moss

You are all so appreciated!

Finally, thank you to all of the amazing people who supported the book during its pre-sale and helped me achieve the goal I needed to fund the publication of the book. All of the people thanked above were supporters of the book, but so were all of these wonderful humans:

- Gregory Bowers
- Jan Wolter
- Rayssa Laberge
- Nevena Pehar
- Jeanmarie Mercado
- Andrew Hrabe
- Aryn Ricardo
- Robert Brzezinski
- Magdalena Stoyantcheva
- Alisa Causevic
- Vesna Rajic
- Morgan Reese
- Maria Theoharis
- Garrett Oswald
- Tyler Wetherill
- Jermaine Evans

- Melinda Dao
- Dylan Connolly
- Joshua Barillas
- Sinisa Milojevic
- Lauren Schafer
- Jacob Westerfield
- Ljubisa Krekic
- Demetrius Roquemore
- Adam Debes
- Emily Jackson
- Brett Post
- Michael Harrison
- Aamer Shareef
- Diana Perez
- Scott Segal
- Brenda Sandonato
- Ruby Jackson
- Dede Yocum
- Gary Gray
- Mohammed Abukhdeir
- Alexa Bertrand
- Bridget Islas
- Mariah Schrotenboer
- Stephanie Depue
- Julio Calderon
- Vy Nguyen
- Ali Sayed
- Naida Adian
- Charles Haselton
- Alexis Soros
- Irene Rodriguez
- Mike Milky

- Jacki Needham
- Vanessa Londono
- Brian Paluck
- Gregg Morton
- Akiem Arthurton
- Abel Arzu
- Zain Husain
- Padma Gordon
- Heather Wilbanks
- Medina Pasalic
- Christie Morales
- Tim Merritt
- Ashlee Rolheiser
- Ke-Erica Hayes
- Carli Walko
- Samantha Maxwell
- Kristen Freda
- Eleanor Pearce
- Ibrahim Jaber
- Natalie Corbin
- Luc Oliver
- Esha Sharda
- Robyn Kibler
- Michelle & Nelson Ruiz
- Moneer K
- Melissa Fumano
- Candace Cruz
- Tulsi Patel
- Maggie Lough
- Nanda Bose
- Scott Tavlin
- Rita Mouradian

- Josh Wilson
- Nicole Denicola
- Daniela Carrasco
- Sead Dizdarevic
- Anthony Swinford
- Dana Barnett
- Snithda Delp

I couldn't have done it without you!

And finally, a big thank you to New Degree Press for all of your work and guidance in the publishing journey!

APPENDIX

INTRODUCTION

World Health Organization. "Depression." World Health Organization. Accessed April 15, 2020. https://www.who.int/news-room/fact-sheets/detail/depression

CHAPTER 1: THE BRAIN 101

Ackerman, MSc, Courtney E. "What Is Neuroplasticity? A Psychologist Explains [+14 Exercises]." Body & Brain. Positive-Psychology.com. April 28, 2020. https://positivepsychology.com/neuroplasticity/

Bouchez, Colette. "Serotonin and Depression: 9 Questions and Answers." WebMD. WebMD LLC. October 12, 2011. https://www.webmd.com/depression/features/serotonin#1.

Harvard Health Publishing. "The Gut-Brain Connection." Healthbeat. Harvard University. Accessed May 1, 2020. https://www.health.harvard.edu/diseases-and-conditions/the-gut-brain-connection

Hoffman, MD, Matthew. "Picture of the Brain: Human Anatomy." WebMD. WebMD LLC. Accessed on May 18, 2020. https://www.webmd.com/brain/picture-of-the-brain#1

Honan, Daniel. "Neuroplasticity: You Can Teach an Old Brain New Tricks." Big Think. The Big Think, Inc. October 11, 2012. https://bigthink.com/think-tank/brain-exercise

Huang, MD, PhD, Juebin. "Overview of Cerebral Function - Neurologic Disorders." Merck Manuals Professional Version. Merck. Accessed May 1, 2020. https://www.merckmanuals.com/professional/neurologic-disorders/function-and-dysfunction-of-the-cerebral-lobes/overview-of-cerebral-function

Isaacson, R. L. "Limbic System." ScienceDirect Topics. International Encyclopedia of the Social & Behavioral Sciences. Accessed May 1, 2020. https://www.sciencedirect.com/topics/neuroscience/limbic-system

Lillard, Angeline S, and Erisir, Alev. "Old Dogs Learning New Tricks: Neuroplasticity Beyond the Juvenile Period." Developmental Review (Volume 31, Issue 4, December 1, 2011). doi: 10.1016/j.dr.2011.07.008

Merriam-Webster. s.v. "neurology (_n._)" Accessed April 30, 2020. https://www.merriam-webster.com/dictionary/neurology

Merriam-Webster. s.v. "psychology (_n._)" Accessed April 30, 2020. https://www.merriam-webster.com/dictionary/psychology

Moawad, MD, Heidi. "How the Brain Processes Emotions." Neurology Times. MJH Life Sciences. June 5, 2017. https://www.neurologytimes.com/blog/how-brain-processes-emotions.

Oxford Reference. s.v. "neuroplasticity (_n._)" Accessed April 20, 2020. https://www.oxfordreference.com/view/10.1093/oi/authority.20110803100230276.

Rosenthal, Michele. "The Science behind PTSD Symptoms: How Trauma Changes The Brain." PsychCentral. Psych Central. June 27, 2019. https://psychcentral.com/blog/the-science-behind-ptsd-symptoms-how-trauma-changes-the-brain/

Shah, Nisheeth. *Left and Right Neural Networks—Inspired by Our Bicameral Brains.* ResearchGate, 2019, fig. 2. Retrieved from https://www.researchgate.net/figure/The-four-lobes-in-the-cerebral-cortex-frontal-lobe-parietal-lobe-temporal-lobe-and_fig2_337186250

Stoller-Conrad, Jessica. "Microbes Help Produce Serotonin in Gut." Caltech. California Institute of Technology. April 9, 2015. https://www.caltech.edu/about/news/microbes-help-produce-serotonin-gut-46495.

Chapter 2: You Against The World

Cherry, Kendra. "Individualistic Cultures and Behavior." Verywell Mind. Dotdash Publishing Family. Reviewed on March 24, 2020. https://www.verywellmind.com/what-are-individualistic-cultures-2795273.

Cherry, Kendra. "Understanding Collectivist Cultures." Verywell Mind. Dotdash Publishing Family. Reviewed on March 24, 2020. https://www.verywellmind.com/what-are-collectivistic-cultures-2794962.

Rosenbaum, Ava. "Personal Space and American Individualism." Brown Political Review. Brown University. October 31, 2018. http://brownpoliticalreview.org/2018/10/personal-space-american-individualism/

Chapter 3: Stigma And Survival

Adams, Tim. "Good Reasons for Bad Feelings Review—a New Approach to Mental Disorder." Review of *Good Reasons for Bad Feelings* by Randolph Nesse. *The Guardian*, March 17, 2019. https://www.theguardian.com/books/2019/mar/17/good-reasons-for-bad-feelings-review-randolph-nesse

Oxford. s.v. "stigma (_n._)" Accessed on April 30, 2020. http://english.oxforddictionaries.com/stigma

CHAPTER 4: SOON YOU'LL GET BETTER: THE TOOLS

"DSM–5 Educational Resources." American Psychiatric Association. American Psychiatric Association. Accessed May 3, 2020. https://www.psychiatry.org/psychiatrists/practice/dsm/educational-resources.

Parekh, MD, Ranna. "What Are Anxiety Disorders?" American Psychiatric Association. American Psychiatric Association. January 2017. https://www.psychiatry.org/patients-families/anxiety-disorders/what-are-anxiety-disorders

Parekh, MD, Ranna. "What Are Bipolar Disorders?" American Psychiatric Association. American Psychiatric Association. January 2017. https://www.psychiatry.org/patients-families/bipolar-disorders/what-are-bipolar-disorders

Parekh, MD, Ranna. "What Is Depression?" American Psychiatric Association. American Psychiatric Association. January 2017. https://www.psychiatry.org/patients-families/depression/what-is-depression

Parekh, MD, Ranna. "What Is Mental Illness?" American Psychiatric Association. American Psychiatric Association, August 2018. https://www.psychiatry.org/patients-families/what-is-mental-illness

Shelley, Taylor. "Coping Strategies." MacArthur | Research Network on SES & Health. University of California, San Francisco. July 1998. https://www.macses.ucsf.edu/research/psychosocial/coping.php.

CHAPTER 10: PEOPLE HAVE RIGHTS, AND YES, IT'S INCONVENIENT

King Jr., Martin Luther. *Quotations of Martin Luther King Jr.* Carlisle, MA: Applewood Books, 2004.

"Universal Declaration of Human Rights." United Nations: Peace, dignity and equality on a healthy planet. United Nations.

Accessed May 16, 2020. https://www.un.org/en/universal-declaration-human-rights/

CHAPTER 13: KINDNESS IS ALWAYS THE ANSWER, BUT THAT DOESN'T ALWAYS MEAN BEING NICE

"The 2019 Florida Statutes: Chapter 394: Mental Health." Statutes & Constitution: View Statutes: Online Sunshine. The Florida Legislature. Accessed on May 14, 2020. http://www.leg.state.fl.us/statutes/index.cfm?App_mode=Display_Statute&URL=0300-0399/0394/0394.html

CHAPTER 19: 'A BIG FAT PHONY'

"Facts & Statistics." Anxiety and Depression Association of America. ADAA. 2018. https://adaa.org/about-adaa/press-room/facts-statistics

Lexico Dictionaries powered by Oxnard. s.v. "Impostor Syndrome (_n._)" Accessed May 8, 2020. https://www.lexico.com/en/definition/impostor_syndrome

Sakulku, Jaruwan. "The Impostor Phenomenon." *The Journal of Behavioral Science* (6 (1), September 2011). https://doi.org/10.14456/ijbs.2011.6

CHAPTER 20: THE IMPORTANCE OF CONTEXT

Anderson, Janna, and Lee Rainie. "Millennials Will Benefit and Suffer Due to Their Hyperconnected Lives." Pew Research Center: Internet & Technology. The Pew Charitable Trusts, February 29, 2012. https://www.pewresearch.org/internet/2012/02/29/millennials-will-benefit-and-suffer-due-to-their-hyperconnected-lives/

Shensa, Ariel, Jaime E Sidani, Mary Amanda Dew, César G Escobar-Viera, and Brian A Primack. "Social Media Use and Depression and Anxiety Symptoms: A Cluster Analysis."

American Journal of Health Behavior (Volume 42, Issue 2, March 2018). doi: 10.5993/AJHB.42.2.11

www.ingramcontent.com/pod-product-compliance
Lightning Source LLC
LaVergne TN
LVHW011808060526
838200LV00053B/3700